crepes crepes crepes
pes crepes crepes
crepes crepes crepe
epes crepes crepe
s crepes crepes cr
es crepes crepes c
epes crepes crepe

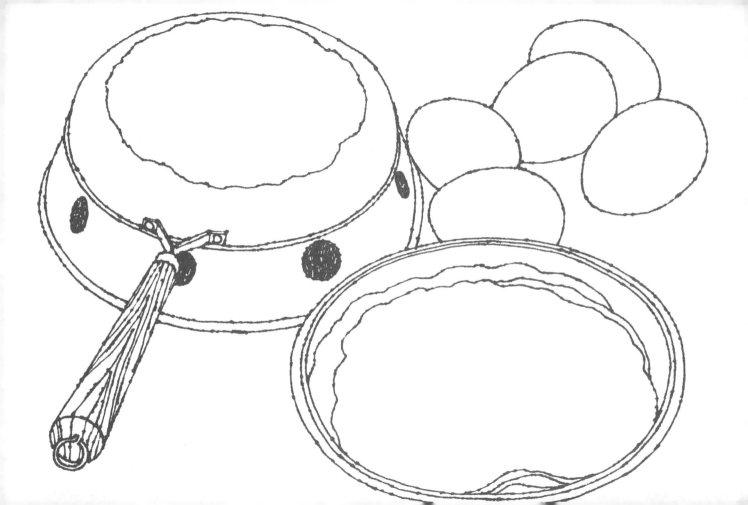

crepes
& omelets

by BOB and COLEEN SIMMONS

Illustrated by CRAIG TORLUCCI

A Nitty Gritty Book*
Published by
Nitty Gritty Productions
P.O. Box 5457
Concord, California 94524

*Nitty Gritty Books - Trademark
Owned by Nitty Gritty Productions
Concord, California

ISBN 0-911954-35-X

TABLE OF CONTENTS

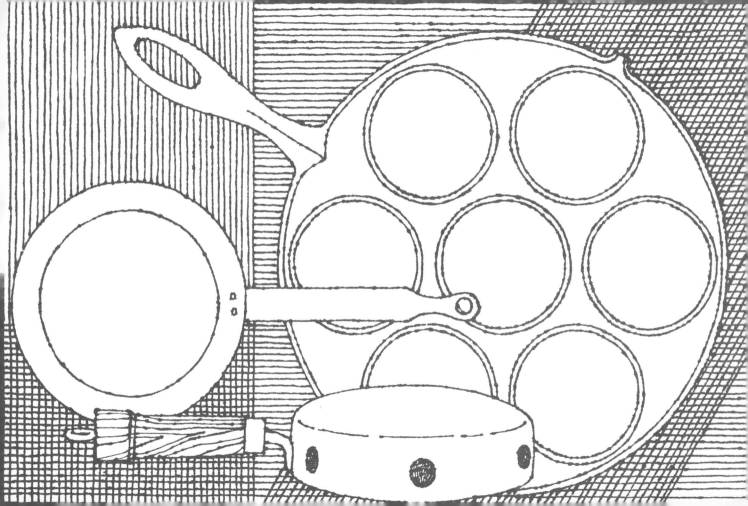

ALL ABOUT CREPES

Crepes are thin pancakes which the French use with marvelous versatility. Because of their association with French cooking, crepes have had the reputation of being mysterious and complicated. Actually they are easy to make and look elegant while being extremely economical and versatile. The difference between a pancake and a crepe is primarily consistency. Crepes use only eggs for leavening and are made as thin as possible so they can be rolled around a filling, while a pancake tends to be puffier and more substantial. Crepes can be wrapped around delightful combinations of meat, poultry or fish and covered with a sauce for luncheon or dinner entrees fit for royalty, or they can be filled with yesterday's leftover chicken and covered with a simple sauce for a quick dinner entree on a busy day.

A vegetable crepe can be used to complement almost any entree, and dessert crepes, from those with simple fruit fillings to elegant Crepes Suzette, can provide the final touch to a gourmet dinner.

Crepes are great time savers because they keep well in the refrigerator or freezer and can be made ahead in quantity and used as needed.

Classic Pans and Skillets

The classic crepe pan used for making main course crepes measures 6 to 7 inches in diameter, while the pans for dessert crepes are generally smaller, about 4 to 5 inches in diameter. Use whichever size you prefer. If you make the smaller crepes for a main course dish, you may wish to serve three crepes rather than the usual two per serving of the larger size. The classic crepe pan is made of medium weight, mild steel with a flat bottom and sloping sides for ease of turning the crepe. Detailed instructions for seasoning and using these traditional pans are given in the Classic Crepes Recipe, beginning on page 5.

Teflon-lined crepe pans work well if properly cared for. The best of the no-stick cookware are the T-Fal pans. They have a more durable Teflon-type finish and it is possible to make crepes in these pans using a light coating of butter or oil for the first crepe only. T-Fal pans come in several sizes. The large ones are excellent for making the extra large crepes needed for egg rolls and blintzes.

If you plan to use a small skillet which has not been reserved for omelets or crepes only, care should be taken to prepare it and prevent its sticking. There are several no-stick spray shortenings available which are excellent for converting a skillet into a crepe or omelet pan. Spray the pan, heat it and use a little butter or oil for the first couple of crepes. If the first crepes do not turn out perfectly or are difficult to remove from the pan, don't be discouraged. It may be necessary to cook a few crepes before the pan is seasoned and at the right temperature. Just keep adding a little more butter or oil to the pan before you start the next crepe. The combination of heat and fat will finally season the pan and it will make excellent crepes.

Crepe Griddles

There are several new crepe devices on the market which are called crepe makers or crepe griddles. The crepes are cooked on the outside of the curved griddle and are extremely light and thin and do not have to be turned. These special devices are easy to use once they are properly prepared. To season, rub the curved surface with a little oil then heat it over low heat for approximately 30 minutes, or for the time specified by the manufacturer. Wipe off any excess oil

3

and the griddle is ready to use. Apply a thin coat of oil or butter each time you start to make crepes. Have crepe batter in a shallow pan, or plate, that will accommodate the curved part of the griddle so as much of it as possible will be covered with batter. Heat the crepe griddle over medium heat until a few drops of water will bounce or sputter on it. Dip griddle into batter. Lift out immediately and place batter side up over heat. Cook approximately 20 to 30 seconds until crepe becomes a little crisp or curls slightly around the edge. Invert crepe maker over a plate or piece of foil and let the crepe drop onto it. Continue until all the batter is used. <u>All of the crepe recipes in this book can be used with these new crepe makers.</u> However, a standard crepe pan is preferred for making blintzes or crepes to be deep fried, because those made with a crepe maker are more fragile.

The Classic Crepes Recipe which follows gives detailed directions for making crepes with or without a blender. The preparation and use of the standard crepe pan is covered for those who do not have a crepe griddle. Detailed information about crepe griddles is given in this section beginning on page 3.

CLASSIC CREPES RECIPE

This recipe makes 14 to 16 6-inch crepes or 18 to 22 5-inch crepes.

2 eggs
2 tbs. melted butter or salad oil
1-1/3 cups milk
1 cup all-purpose flour
1/2 tsp. salt

If using a blender: **Place ingredients in the blender container in the order listed. Cover and blend at high speed 20 to 30 seconds. Scrape down sides of container. Blend a few more seconds. *Crepe batter made in a blender can be used immediately,* or refrigerated until needed. If it thickens on standing, thin to the right consistency with a little milk. Crepe batter should be thin enough to run freely around the bottom of the crepe pan when it is tilted.**

If not using a blender: **Beat eggs, milk and oil with rotary egg beater or electric mixer until blended. Gradually add dry ingredients and beat until well mixed and smooth. To be sure that batter is smooth, pour it through a sieve to catch any**

5

lumps which may not have dissolved. _Refrigerate batter 2 hours before cooking crepes._

Pan preparation: If using a no-stick spray shortening, spray pan before heating. Before cooking the first crepe put 1/2 teaspoon butter into pan. If the pan is well seasoned it should not be necessary to add more butter for each crepe. (See instructions for preparing and using crepe griddles on page 3.)

Pan temperature: Crepe pan is at the correct temperature when the batter sizzles slightly when poured into the pan, and a crepe will cook on one side in approximately 1 minute. Crepes should be pale in color, not dark brown.

To cook crepes: Two or three tablespoons of batter is usually enough to cover the bottom of a 6- to 7-inch crepe pan. If necessary, adjust the amount needed for the pan you are using. Pour in the batter and quickly tilt the pan so the batter covers the bottom entirely. If you have put in more than just a thin coating, pour the excess back into the bowl. This will leave a small flap on the crepe but it won't be noticed when the crepe is filled and folded. (Caution: If crepe pan is not hot enough, the whole crepe may fall back into the batter when you pour out the excess. It is important to have the pan at the correct temperature before starting to cook.)

When to turn: The crepe is ready to turn when it begins to set and crisp around the edges. Loosen around the edge with a spatula or knife so you have a starting place to pick up the crepe with your fingers, then simply flip it over. If preferred, carefully turn with a spatula. Should it start to tear when picked up, it may not be cooked enough to turn. Cook a few seconds longer and try again.

If pan sticks in one spot: Put more butter or oil in the pan and wipe with a paper towel. Once a crepe pan is seasoned, it should not be necessary to add more butter or oil for each crepe. It may be necessary to discard the first crepe or two until the pan is properly seasoned and the temperature right. Once a pan is seasoned, never wash or scrub it, just wipe with a paper towel and don't use the pan for anything else, unless you want to have to season it each time it's used.

After the crepes are cooked: Stack cooked crepes on a plate. They will be easier to separate if they are not placed squarely on top of each other. It is not necessary to put foil or waxed paper between each crepe.

Presentation: Crepes can be filled and rolled in a number of ways. See illustrations on page 9.

Crepes Keep Well

Storing: Crepes will keep several days in the refrigerator. Wrap them in foil or plastic.

Freezing: Crepes to be frozen can be stacked right on a piece of foil large enough to be folded over the crepes and tightly sealed. Place foil package in a plastic bag and freeze until needed. It is not necessary to put foil or waxed paper between each crepe. They will pull apart easily when they are defrosted and warmed slightly. Package crepes in the number you will need for a meal, allowing 2 6-inch crepes per serving. If using small ones for main dish crepes, allow 3 per serving. Two 5-inch crepes per serving is enough for desserts unless otherwise specified. Filled crepes do not freeze well in most cases. It is best to freeze crepes and fillings separately.

Defrosting: A foil package of six to eight crepes will defrost in a 350°F oven in 8 to 10 minutes. Carefully separate them while they are still warm.

The first crepes you make may not be perfect, but they will improve with practice. Crepes that are not perfectly round or have a hole where the batter didn't completely fill in will never be noticed when they are filled, rolled and covered with sauce.

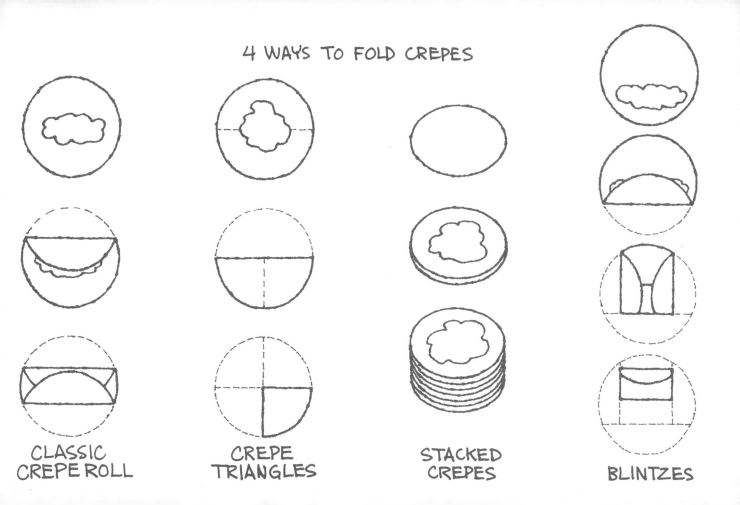

4 WAYS TO FOLD CREPES

CLASSIC CREPE ROLL

CREPE TRIANGLES

STACKED CREPES

BLINTZES

CREPE VARIATIONS AND COMBINATIONS

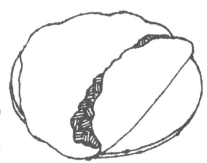

This section begins with a variety of crepes which are combined with various fillings to make such delicious dishes as Chicken and Green Chile Crepes, Lobster Newburg Crepes, Spinach and Ricotta Cheese Crepes, Canneloni and many others.

Use the recipes in this section as a starting point, then increase your enjoyment by trying different crepes with any combination of fillings and sauces that suits your fancy. Make some of your own using whatever is available in the refrigerator or on the pantry shelf. The possibilities will amaze you.

References to the Classic Crepes Recipe on page 5 are made throughout this chapter to be used when necessary as a guide for beginning crepe-makers. After a little practice the basic recipe will be needed only for occasional reference.

Crepes used in main dishes are usually 6 inches in diameter and most recipes allow two crepes for each serving.

BUTTERMILK CREPES

Extra tender and slightly tangy because they're made with buttermilk.

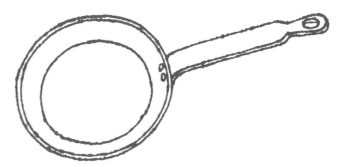

2 eggs
1 cup buttermilk
2 tbs. oil or melted butter
1/3 cup water
1/2 cup sifted cake flour
1/2 cup all-purpose flour
1/2 tsp. salt

Place ingredients in blender container in the order listed. Cover and blend at high speed for 20 to 30 seconds. Scrape down sides of the container. Blend a few more seconds. Cook according to directions given in the Classic Crepe recipe on page 5. Makes 14 to 16 6-inch crepes.

CORN CHIP CREPES

These are similar to corn tortillas and delicious with Mexican-type fillings.

2 eggs
2 tbs. vegetable oil
1 cup milk
1/3 cup water
1/2 cup all-purpose flour
1 cup loosely-packed, crushed Fritos corn chips
1/2 tsp. salt

Place all ingredients in blender container in the order listed. Cover and blend at high speed 20 to 30 seconds. Scrape down sides of the container. Blend a few more seconds. Cook according to directions given in the Classic Crepe recipe on page 5. Stir batter occasionally to prevent Fritos from settling to the bottom. Makes 14 to 16 6-inch crepes.

SPINACH CREPES

A beautiful deep green color to complement any creamy filling.

1/4 cup cooked spinach
2 eggs
1-1/3 cups milk
2 tbs. salad oil or butter
1 cup all-purpose flour
1/2 tsp. salt
3 green onions, chopped
dash white pepper and nutmeg

Drain spinach well and chop. Place eggs, milk, oil or butter, flour and salt in blender container. Cover and blend at high speed until thoroughly combined. Add spinach, onions, pepper and nutmeg. Blend 20 seconds longer. Cook according to directions given in the Classic Crepe recipe on page 5. Makes 14 to 16 6-inch crepes.

WHOLE WHEAT CREPES

For brunch serve with the Curried Egg Filling on page 40, and a fresh fruit compote.

2 eggs
1-1/3 cups milk
2 tbs. salad oil
1 tbs. honey
1 cup whole wheat flour
1/2 tsp. salt

Place ingredients in blender container in the order listed. Cover and blend at high speed for 20 to 30 seconds. Scrape down sides of container. Blend a few more seconds. Cook according to directions given in the Classic Crepes recipe on page 5. Makes 14 to 16 6-inch crepes.

CANNELONI OR MANICOTTI CREPES

2 eggs   3/4 cup water   3/4 cup flour   1/4 tsp. salt

Place ingredients in blender container in order listed. Cover and blend at high speed 20 to 30 seconds. Scrape down sides of container and blend a few more seconds. Cook crepes in a 6- to 7-inch pan according to the directions given for Classic Crepes on page 5. Makes 8 crepes.

EGG ROLL CREPES

2 eggs   1/2 cup water   1/2 tsp. salt
1/3 cup salad oil   1/2 cup flour

Place ingredients in blender container. Cover and blend at high speed 20 to 30 seconds. Scrape down sides of container and blend a few more seconds. Cook crepes in an 8-inch pan according to directions for Classic Crepes, page 5. Makes 6 to 7 crepes.

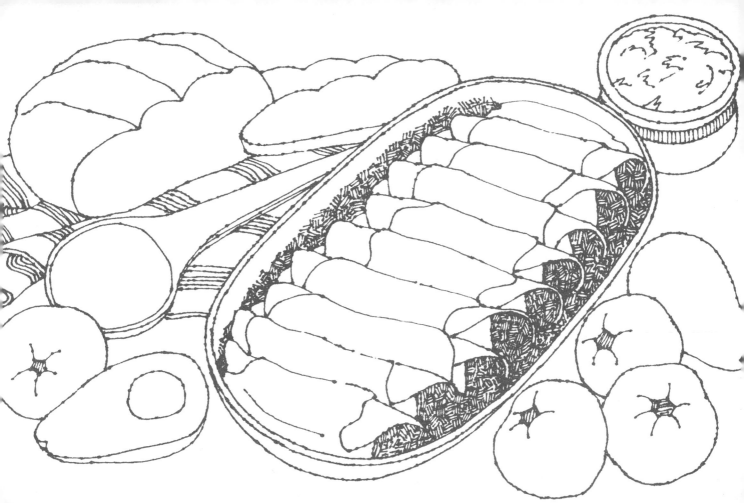

ASPARAGUS AND HAM CREPES

Serve this elegant entree often when asparagus is in season. A fresh pineapple and orange salad makes a perfect accompaniment.

8 Classic Crepes, page 5
8 thin slices ham
16 cooked asparagus spears
1 cup grated Swiss cheese
2 tbs. butter

2 tbs. flour
1-1/4 cups milk
1/2 cup grated Swiss cheese
1/4 tsp. white pepper
1/2 tsp. salt

Make crepes as directed and set aside. Place one slice of ham on each crepe. Top each with 2 asparagus spears and 2 tablespoons grated Swiss cheese. Roll up and place in buttered ovenproof serving dish. Melt butter in small saucepan. Stir in flour and cook 2 minutes. Add milk gradually and cook, stirring, over low heat until sauce thickens. Stir in the remaining 1/2 cup Swiss cheese, pepper and salt. Spoon sauce over rolled crepes. Place in 375°F oven 10 to 15 minutes to heat. Run under broiler to lightly brown. Makes 4 servings.

MUSHROOM AND HAM CREPES

Next time try this filling in a different kind of crepe.

8 Buttermilk Crepes, page 12
1 pound fresh mushrooms
1/4 cup finely minced shallots or green onions
6 tbs. butter
1 cup finely chopped ham
salt and white pepper
1 cup (1/2 pt.) sour cream
Creamy Mustard Sauce, page 63

Make crepes as directed and set aside. Chop mushrooms very finely and combine with shallots. Melt butter in skillet. Add mushrooms and shallots. Saute over high heat 3 to 4 minutes. Add chopped ham, salt and pepper. Cook until mixture is dry. Fold in sour cream just before assembling the crepes. Fill and roll crepes. Place in buttered, ovenproof serving dish. Heat in 350°F oven 10 to 15 minutes. Top with Creamy Mustard Sauce. Makes 4 servings.

CHICKEN AND BROCCOLI CREPES

Chicken divan wrapped in crepes makes a pretty party entree.

8 Classic Crepes, page 5
3 tbs. butter
3 tbs. flour
1-1/2 cups milk
2 tsp. Worcestershire
1-1/2 cups sharp cheese, grated

salt and pepper
2 cups cooked chicken, cubed
8 tbs. sour cream
8 pieces cooked broccoli
Parmesan cheese

Make crepes as directed and set aside. Melt butter in small saucepan. Add flour and cook 2 minutes. Gradually add milk. Cook, stirring, until sauce thickens. Add Worcestershire, cheese, salt and pepper. Stir chicken cubes into sauce. Spread each crepe with 1 tablespoon sour cream. Place a broccoli spear on top of sour cream. Cover broccoli with chicken mixture. Roll up crepes. Place in buttered, ovenproof serving dish. Sprinkle with Parmesan cheese. Heat in 375°F oven 10 to 15 minutes. Makes 4 servings.

CHICKEN AND GREEN CHILE CREPES

Chicken with a Mexican accent is sure to please.

8 Corn Chip Crepes, page 13   1 tbs. chopped pimiento
1/8 tsp. cumin   1/4 cup sliced black olives
3/4 cup sour cream   1 tbs. chopped fresh coriander leaves (optional)
2 cups cooked, cubed chicken   salt and pepper
1 canned green chile, chopped   3/4 cup grated Monterey Jack cheese

Make crepes as directed and set aside. Combine cumin with sour cream in mixing bowl. Add chicken, green chile, pimiento, olives, coriander, salt and pepper. Mix well. Spoon a little of mixture onto each crepe and roll. Placed filled crepes in buttered, ovenproof serving dish or individual dishes. Sprinkle with grated cheese. Heat in 375°F oven 10 minutes. Run under heated broiler to lightly brown. Makes 4 servings.

CURRIED CHICKEN CREPES

A delicate French-style curry accented with avocado and peanuts.

12 Classic Crepes, page 5
2 tbs. butter
2 tbs. flour
1 tsp. curry powder
1 cup milk
salt and white pepper

2-1/2 cups cooked, cubed chicken
1 large avocado, diced
1/3 cup coarsely chopped peanuts
Cream Sauce, page 23
2 to 3 tbs. grated Parmesan cheese

Make crepes as directed and set aside. Melt butter in small saucepan. Stir in flour and curry powder. Cook 2 minutes. Add milk gradually. Cook, stirring until sauce thickens. Season with salt and pepper. Combine chicken with sauce. Spoon some of curried chicken onto each crepe. Add a few pieces of avocado and a generous sprinkling of peanuts to each crepe and roll up. Place in a buttered, ovenproof serving dish. Top filled crepes with cream sauce. Sprinkle with Parmesan. Heat in 350°F oven 10 to 15 minutes until hot and bubbly. Run under broiler to brown top lightly. Makes 6 servings.

Cream Sauce

1/4 cup butter
1/4 cup flour
1 cup milk
1 cup chicken broth
1 tsp. Worcestershire sauce
salt and white pepper

Melt butter in small saucepan over medium heat. Stir in flour and cook, stirring, 2 minutes. Add milk, broth and Worcestershire gradually. Cook, stirring, until sauce thickens. Season with salt and pepper.

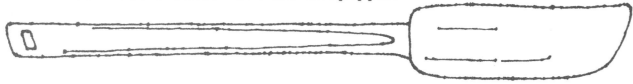

CANNELONI

Canneloni Crepes, page 16
Tomato Sauce, page 25
2 tbs. olive oil
1 carrot, coarsely grated
1 onion, chopped
2 cups cooked chicken

1/3 cup chopped parsley
1/3 cup heavy cream
1 egg
salt and white pepper
Cheese Sauce, page 25
Parmesan cheese

Make crepes as directed and set aside. Mix tomato sauce and let simmer while preparing filling and cheese sauce. To make filling, heat olive oil in skillet. Add carrot and onion and cook until soft but not brown. Put cooked vegetables and diced chicken (or turkey) through the coarse blade of a meat grinder. Stir in parsley, cream, egg, salt and pepper. Set aside. Make cheese sauce last. To complete canneloni, spread crepes with meat mixture and roll. Place seam side down in buttered, ovenproof casserole or individual serving dishes. Top crepes with tomato sauce. Then spoon cheese sauce over tomato sauce. Sprinkle with Parmesan. Heat in 350°F oven 15 minutes or until hot and bubbly. Run under broiler to lightly brown cheese. Makes 4 servings.

24

Tomato Sauce

1 can (15 ozs.) tomato sauce	1/2 tsp. oregano
1/3 cup red wine	1 tsp. sweet basil
salt and pepper	1 garlic clove, minced

Combine ingredients in a small saucepan. Simmer uncovered 25 minutes. Stir occasionally. Use as directed.

Cheese Sauce

2 tbs. butter	1/2 cup grated Swiss cheese
2 tbs. flour	1/2 tsp. salt
1-1/3 cups milk	white pepper, nutmeg

Melt butter in a small saucepan over medium heat. Add flour and cook, stirring, 2 minutes. Gradually blend in milk. Cook, stirring, until sauce thickens. Stir in cheese, salt, pepper and nutmeg. Use as directed.

TURKEY-MUSHROOM-WATER CHESTNUT CREPES

A perfect way to use leftover turkey, as well as chicken or pork.

8 Classic Crepes, page 5
Wine Sauce, page 27
1/4 cup butter
2 cups sliced fresh mushrooms
6 green onions, thinly sliced
1/4 cup chopped pimientos
4 water chestnuts, diced
2 cups diced cooked turkey
paprika

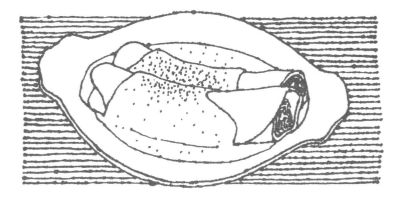

Make crepes and wine sauce as directed. Set both aside until needed. Melt butter in skillet. When foaming add mushrooms. Saute 3 to 4 minutes. Add onions and cook 2 to 3 minutes longer. Add pimientos, chestnuts and turkey. Add just enough of the wine sauce to moisten. Fill crepes with turkey mixture. Roll and place in buttered, ovenproof serving dish, or individual au gratin dishes.

Top with remaining wine sauce. Sprinkle with paprika. Heat in 375°F oven 10 minutes then run under broiler to lightly brown the top. Makes 4 servings.

Wine Sauce

1/4 cup butter
1/4 cup flour
1/4 cup dry sherry or vermouth
2 cups milk
1 tbs. Worcestershire sauce
salt, white pepper

Melt butter in small saucepan over medium heat. Add flour and cook, stirring 2 minutes. Gradually add sherry, milk, Worcestershire, salt and pepper. Cook, stirring, until sauce thickens. Use as directed.

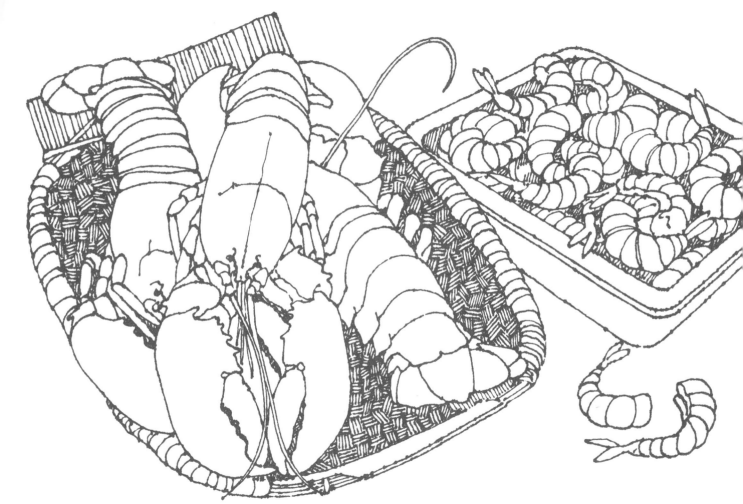

LOBSTER NEWBURG CREPES

An elegant first course for a dinner party, or a substantial luncheon for four. Also good with shrimp or crab.

12 Classic Crepes, page 5
2 tbs. butter
1/4 cup flour
1-1/2 cups heavy cream
1/2 cup milk

3 egg yolks
1/4 cup dry sherry
salt and pepper
2-1/2 cups cooked lobster

Make Classic Crepes as directed and set aside. Melt butter in top of double boiler over simmering water. Stir in flour and cook 2 to 3 minutes. Gradually add cream and milk. Cook, stirring occasionally until sauce thickens. Mix a little of the hot cream mixture into egg yolks. Carefully stir egg yolk mixture into sauce. Blend in sherry, salt and pepper. Add lobster and heat through. Fill crepes, reserving some of the sauce for the top of the crepes. Roll and place in buttered, ovenproof serving dishes. Top with the reserved sauce. Place in 350°F oven 10 to 15 minutes, or until heated through. Makes 6 servings.

PORK AND GREEN CHILE CREPES

A snappy dish that is sure to please.

1 tbs. butter
1 small onion, chopped
2 cups cubed cooked pork
1 can (4 ozs.) diced green chiles, undrained
1 tsp. salt

1/4 tsp. pepper
3/4 cup water
12 Corn Chip Crepes, page 13
3 to 4 drops Tabasco
1 tbs. each butter and flour

Melt butter in frying pan. Saute onion until soft. Add cooked pork, chiles and juice, salt, pepper and water. Cover and simmer over medium heat for 30 minutes until mixture has thickened slightly. While sauce simmers, make crepes as directed and set aside. Blend butter and flour together. Taste sauce and if desired add Tabasco sauce. Gradually add butter-flour mixture to sauce to thicken. Spoon some of the filling on each crepe and roll. Place rolled crepes in a buttered, ovenproof serving dish or individual dishes. heat in 375°F oven 10 minutes. Run under broiler to lightly brown. Makes 6 servings.

CREPES A LA STROGANOFF

1 lb. round steak
1/2 lb. fresh mushrooms
4 tbs. butter
1/2 cup chopped onion
2 medium tomatoes
1 clove garlic, minced

1 tsp. salt
1 tbs. Worcestershire sauce
6 drops Tabasco
1/8 tsp. pepper
8 Classic Crepes, page 5
1-1/4 cups sour cream

Cut steak into 1/2- x 1-inch strips. Thinly slice mushrooms and saute in 2 tablespoons butter. Remove from pan and set aside. Add remaining butter to pan. Brown meat and onion together over high heat. Stir constantly. Peel, seed and chop tomatoes. Add tomatoes, garlic, salt, Worcestershire, Tabasco and pepper to meat. Cover and simmer 30 to 40 minutes. While meat simmers, make crepes as directed. When meat is tender add 1 cup sour cream and just heat through. Spoon a small amount of meat mixture onto each crepe. Roll and place in buttered, ovenproof serving dish. Run under hot broiler 2 to 3 minutes. Top each crepe with a spoonful of sour cream. Makes 4 servings.

BEEF PAPRIKA CREPES

A hearty old favorite dressed up in a crepe makes a delicious party dish which can be prepared in advance and heated just before serving.

1 lb. top beef round, 3/4-in. thick
2 tbs. butter
1 large onion, chopped
1 medium green pepper, chopped
1-1/2 tbs. Hungarian sweet red paprika
1 large tomato
1-1/2 cups dry red wine
1 tbs. sugar
1/2 tsp. salt
8 Classic Crepes, page 5
1 cup (1/2 pt.) sour cream
sour cream for topping

Cut beef into 1/4- x 1-inch strips. Melt butter in a flameproof casserole with

a tight-fitting lid. Saute beef strips in butter. Remove when browned. Add onion, green pepper and paprika to casserole. Saute 2 to 3 minutes, adding more butter if necessary. Peel, seed and chop tomato. Add to casserole with red wine and sugar. Return meat to casserole. Add salt and stir. Bring to boil on top of stove. Cover tightly and place in a 275°F oven about 2 hours or until meat is tender. Check after 1 hour. Add more water or wine if necessary. While meat cooks make crepes as directed and set aside. When meat is tender stir in sour cream. Fill crepes with meat mixture and roll. Place in ovenproof serving dish. If serving immediately, run under the broiler to crisp the crepes. If reheating is necessary, place in 375°F oven 10 to 15 minutes. Then run under the broiler to lightly brown. Top crepes with a dollop of sour cream and sprinkle with a little more red paprika. Makes 4 servings.

Pork Paprika Crepes: Substitute pork for the beef.

MEXICAN CREPES

Corn Chip Crepes filled with chili flavored meat and cheddar cheese, topped with a sauce of fresh tomatoes and avocados.

8 Corn Chip Crepes, page 13
3/4 lb. ground beef
1/4 cup catsup
1/4 tsp. dry mustard
1/4 tsp. chili powder

1 tbs. taco sauce
1/2 cup water
salt and pepper
1 cup grated cheddar cheese
Tomato Avocado Sauce, page 35

Make crepes as directed and set aside. Saute meat in skillet. When browned and finely crumbled, drain off excess fat. Add catsup, mustard, chili powder, taco sauce, salt and pepper. Pour in 1/2 cup water. Simmer on low heat, uncovered, until mixture is quite dry.

Fill Corn Chip Crepes with meat mixture. Sprinkle cheddar cheese on meat mixture. Roll crepes, place in lightly greased, ovenproof serving dish. Heat at 350°F for 10 to 15 minutes until crepes are hot. Serve with Tomato Avocado Sauce. Makes 4 servings.

Tomato Avocado Sauce

2 ripe avocados
2 ripe tomatoes
2 to 3 green onions
4 to 5 tbs. chopped fresh cilantro
1/2 tsp. salt
pepper to taste

Peel, seed and dice avocados and tomatoes. Thinly slice green onions. Combine avocados, tomatoes, green onions, cilantro, salt and pepper. Let stand at room temperature 20 to 30 minutes before serving so mixture becomes juicy. Stir occasionally. Makes sauce for 8 crepes.

Note: Mexican Crepes freeze well. Fill crepes, place in foil pan, cover and freeze. To defrost, place foil covered pan in 375°F oven 30 to 35 minutes.

 **MANICOTTI**

A popular dish of cheese filled crepes topped with an Italian sauce.

Tomato Sauce, page 37
Manicotti Crepes, page 16
1/2 lb. mozzarella cheese, grated
1/2 lb. ricotta cheese
salt and pepper
1 egg
1/2 cup diced ham (optional)

Make tomato sauce as directed. While it is simmering, make crepes and set aside. To make filling combine mozzarella, ricotta, salt, pepper, egg and ham. Spread filling mixture on crepes. Roll and place seam side down in buttered, ovenproof casserole or individual serving dishes. Top with tomato sauce. Place in 350°F oven 15 minutes or until hot and bubbly. Makes 4 servings.

Tomato Sauce

1 can (15 ozs.) tomato sauce with tomato pieces
1/3 cup red wine
salt and pepper
1-1/2 tsp. Italian herb seasoning
1 garlic clove, minced
2 tbs. butter
6 to 8 fresh mushrooms, sliced

Combine tomato sauce, wine, salt, pepper, Italian seasoning and garlic in a small saucepan. Simmer 20 to 25 minutes to blend flavors. Melt butter in small skillet. Saute fresh mushrooms 4 to 5 minutes over high heat. Add mushrooms to cooked sauce. Use as directed.

SPINACH AND RICOTTA CHEESE CREPES

A marvelous blending of flavors you'll want to enjoy often.

8 Classic Crepes, page 5
1 pkg. (10 ozs.) frozen chopped spinach
1 tbs. butter
1/2 cup onion, finely chopped
1 cup ricotta cheese
2 tbs. grated Parmesan cheese
1/3 cup light cream
salt, pepper, dash nutmeg
1/2 cup diced ham or proscuitto
Cheese Sauce, page 39

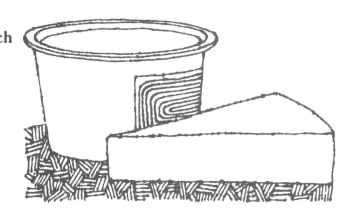

Make crepes as directed and set aside. Cook spinach according to package instructions. Drain and squeeze as dry as possible. Chop coarsely to break up the strings. Set aside. Melt butter in large saucepan. Saute onion 5 to 6 minutes until soft but not brown. Stir in spinach, ricotta and Parmesan. Mix well. Add cream and seasonings. Fold in ham or proscuitto. Fill and roll crepes. Place in buttered, ovenproof serving dish or individual au gratin dishes. Top with cheese sauce. Heat in 375°F oven until brown and bubbly. Makes 4 servings.

Cheese Sauce

2 tbs. butter
2 tbs. flour
1-1/4 cups milk
1 tsp. Worcestershire sauce
1/3 cup grated Parmesan cheese
salt and white pepper

Melt butter in a small saucepan over medium heat. Add flour and cook, stirring, 2 minutes. Gradually blend in milk. Cook, stirring, until sauce thickens. Add Worcestershire, cheese, salt and pepper. Heat through. Serve on Spinach and Ricotta Cheese Crepes.

CURRIED EGG CREPES

Serve with chutney for the perfect finishing touch.

8 Whole Wheat Crepes, page 15
1/4 cup butter
1/4 cup flour
1 tsp. curry powder

2-1/2 cups milk
1 tsp. salt
white pepper
6 hard-cooked eggs, chopped

Make crepes as directed and set aside. Melt butter in small saucepan. Stir in flour and curry powder. Cook 2 minutes. Gradually blend in milk and cook, stirring over low heat until sauce thickens. Season with salt and pepper. Add just enough curry sauce to the hard-cooked eggs to moisten them. Place a small amount of egg filling on each crepe. Roll and place in buttered, ovenproof serving dish. Spread rolled crepes with remaining curry sauce. Place under broiler until lightly browned and bubbly. Makes 4 servings.

Variation: Small shrimps or diced chicken can be added to, or substituted for, the eggs.

40

CUCUMBER AND MUSHROOM CREPES

Serve these as a vegetable course with salmon or red snapper.

8 Classic Crepes, page 5
1 long English cucumber, or 2 regular cucumbers
salt
2 tbs. butter
6 to 8 fresh mushrooms, coarsely chopped
1/4 tsp. dill weed
pepper
2 to 3 tbs. sour cream

Make crepes as directed and set aside. Peel, cut in half and seed cucumber if necessary. Cut into 1/4-inch slices. Sprinkle with salt and let stand 20 minutes. Rinse off salt and pat dry. Melt butter in skillet. Add cucumbers, mushrooms, dill and pepper. Saute 10 minutes or until vegetables are soft. Stir in enough sour cream to moisten. Fill crepes. Place in buttered, ovenproof serving dish. Heat in 375°F oven 8 to 10 minutes. Serve immediately. Makes 6 servings.

STACKED CREPE SANDWICH

Vary this unusual sandwich with different combinations of fillings.

12 Classic Crepes, page 5	**5 to 7 slices mild cheese**
1 ripe avocado	**5 to 7 slices cooked ham**
2 whole pimientos	**5 to 7 slices salami**
1/2 cup mayonnaise	**5 to 7 slices mortadella**
2 tbs. prepared mustard	**olives, cherry tomatoes, pickles**

Make crepes as directed and set aside. Peel and thinly slice avocado. Cut pimientos into inch-wide strips. Combine mayonnaise and mustard. Spread each crepe with some of the mixture. Place 2 or 3 slices of meat or cheese on each of 9 crepes, alternating the different kinds. Stack as you go. Make a layer each of the avocado slices and pimiento strips. The last crepe should be placed mayonnaise side down on the top. Poke 4 skewers through stack. Refrigerate for an hour. Skewer olives, tomatoes and pickles on toothpicks to garnish each serving. Cut into wedges and serve. Makes 4 servings.

CHILI DOG CREPES

Wieners and chili in Corn Chip Crepes, topped with cheese. A quick supper combination sure to receive approval.

8 Corn Chip Crepes, page 13
2 cans (15 ozs.) chili without beans
8 wieners
2 cups (1/2 lb.) grated cheddar cheese

Make crepes as directed. Heat chili in a small saucepan. Place a wiener on each crepe. Top with a small amount of chili. Sprinkle with cheese. Roll and place in buttered, ovenproof serving dish. Top rolled crepes with remaining chili and cover with remaining cheese. Place under broiler until cheese melts. Makes 4 servings.

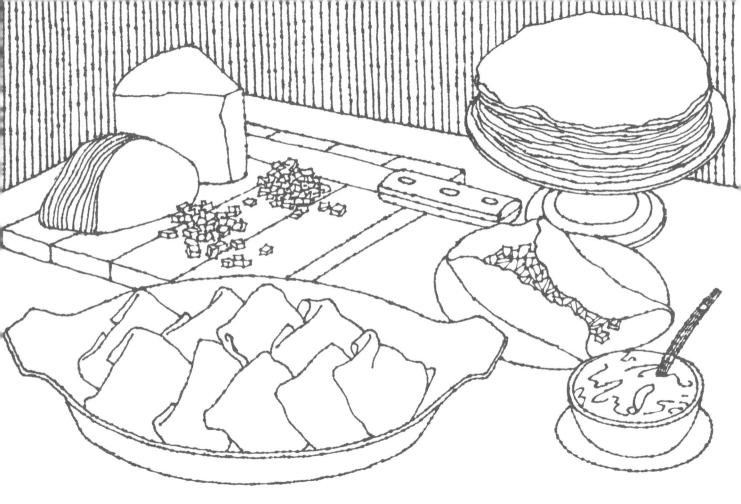

BLINTZES AND OTHER SPECIALTIES

Blintzes for brunch. A great idea because everything can be prepared ahead of time. Have a stack of crepes and a choice of fillings ready and make blintzes to each guest's order. Fill and fold, then saute the blintzes right at the table in an electric skillet. When delicately browned and heated, serve with sour cream.

Try Crepe Cups on page 58 for a new way of serving crepes. Crepes are used instead of pastry for making tarts. Baked with a quiche or souffle filling, they are delicious and attractive. Crepe Cups make a delightful appetizer course for a dinner party and are sure to bring raves from your guests. And a dessert souffle filling baked in a Crepe Cup makes a light but impressive ending to a lovely meal.

BASIC BLINTZES

Blintzes are crepes with a special fold which àre fried in butter and oil just before serving. Small blintzes make great appetizers.

3 eggs	1/2 tsp. salt
1-1/4 cups milk	3 tbs. butter
2 tbs. melted butter	1 tbs. salad oil
1 cup all-purpose flour	

Place ingredients in blender container in the order listed. Cover and blend at high speed 20 to 30 seconds. Scrape down sides of container. Blend a few more seconds. Cook blintzes in a 7- to 8-inch crepe pan (larger blintzes are easier to fill and roll) according to directions for Classic Crepes on page 5. See diagrams on page 9 for filling and rolling. When ready to serve, heat butter and oil in a large skillet. Saute the rolled blintzes approximately 2 to 3 minutes on each side until they are golden brown. Drain on paper toweling. Serve hot. Makes 12 to 14 large blintzes.

BEEF BLINTZES

8 Basic Blintzes, page 46
1/2 lb. ground beef
1 tbs. butter or oil
1 small onion, finely chopped
1/3 cup water
1 tsp. prepared mustard

1 tbs. Worcestershire sauce
2 to 3 tbs. sour cream
1 hard-cooked egg, finely chopped
salt and pepper
3 tbs. butter
1 tbs. salad oil

Make crepes as directed and set aside. Brown meat in skillet, crumbling it into small pieces. Drain and set aside. Melt butter in skillet and saute onion over low heat. After onion has cooked 3 to 4 minutes, add 1/3 cup water. Cook until water evaporates and onion is soft. Combine meat, onion, mustard, Worcestershire, sour cream, hard-cooked egg, salt and pepper. See diagram on page 9 for filling and rolling the blintzes. When ready to serve, heat butter and oil in large skillet. Fry rolled blintzes 2 to 3 minutes on each side until golden brown. Drain on paper toweling and serve hot. Makes 8 large blintzes.

CHICKEN AND GREEN CHILE BLINTZES

4 Basic Blintzes, page 46
2 tbs. finely chopped canned green chiles
1 cup diced cooked chicken
2 to 3 tbs. sour cream
salt and pepper
3 tbs. butter
1 tbs. salad oil

Make crepes as directed and set aside. Rinse green chiles under cold water and remove seeds before chopping. Combine chopped chiles with chicken and enough sour cream just to moisten. Season with salt and pepper. See diagram on page 9 for filling and rolling the blintzes. When ready to serve heat butter and oil in large skillet. Fry rolled blintzes 2 to 3 minutes on each side until golden brown. Drain on paper toweling and serve hot. Makes 4 large blintzes.

PASTRAMI BLINTZES

6 Basic Blintzes, page 46
2 cups diced pastrami
3 tbs. prepared mustard
3 to 4 tbs. heavy cream
3 tbs. butter
1 tbs. salad oil

Make crepes as directed and set aside. Combine pastrami, mustard and enough cream to moisten pastrami. See diagram on page 9 for filling and rolling the blintzes. When ready to serve, heat butter and oil in large skillet. Fry rolled blintzes 2 to 3 minutes on each side until golden brown. Drain on paper toweling and serve hot with Creamy Mustard Sauce on page 63. Makes 6 large blintzes.

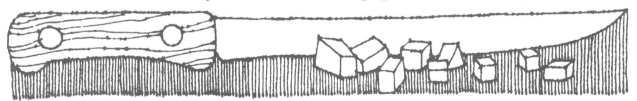

TUNA BLINTZES

This makes a good luncheon dish.

6 Basic Blintzes, page 46
5 or 6 green onions
1 tbs. butter
1 can (6 ozs.) tuna, drained
1/4 tsp. celery salt

pepper
1/2 cup (2 ozs.) grated cheddar cheese
1 egg
3 tbs. butter
1 tbs. salad oil

Make crepes as directed and set aside. Thinly slice green onions and saute in butter until soft. Stir in tuna, celery salt, pepper, cheese and egg. Cook 2 to 3 minutes. See diagram on page 8 for filling and rolling the blintzes. When ready to serve, heat butter and oil in large skillet. Fry rolled blintzes 2 to 3 minutes on each side until golden brown. Drain on paper toweling and serve hot. Makes 6 large blintzes.

CHEESE DESSERT BLINTZES

Vary the filling by adding drained, cooked apples, cherries or blueberries.

6 Basic Blintzes, page 46
1 cup (1/2 pt.) small curd creamed cottage cheese
1 pkg. (3 ozs.) Philadelphia cream cheese
1/4 cup sour cream
2 tbs. sugar
grated lemon rind
3 tbs. butter
1 tbs. salad oil

Make crepes as directed. Set aside. Place cottage cheese, cream cheese, sour cream, sugar and lemon rind in blender container. Blend on high speed until mixture is smooth and creamy. Add cooked fruit if desired. See diagram on page 9 for filling and rolling the blintzes. Heat butter and oil in large skillet. Fry filled blintzes 2 to 3 minutes each side until they are golden brown. Drain on paper toweling and serve hot. Makes 6 large blintzes.

CHEESE AND APPLE BLINTZES

Cheese and apple filling is also good in plain or walnut crepes.

8 Basic Blintzes, page 46
2 tbs. butter
2 med. cooking apples
3 tbs. brown sugar
1/2 cup water

1/2 tsp. vanilla
1/4 tsp. cinnamon
Cheese Filling, page 51
3 tbs. butter
1 tbs. salad oil

Make crepes as directed and set aside. Heat butter in medium skillet. Peel and thinly slice apples. Saute apples in butter 4 to 5 minutes until they are well glazed. Add sugar, water, vanilla and cinnamon. Cook uncovered for about 10 minutes until water has evaporated and mixture is soft. Place 2 tablespoons Cheese Filling in center of each blintz crepe. Top with an equal amount of apple filling. See diagram on page 9 for rolling the blintzes. Heat butter and oil in large skillet. Fry the filled blintzes 2 to 3 minutes on each side until they are golden brown. Drain on paper toweling and serve hot. Makes 8 blintzes.

EGG ROLLS

Serve with Mustard Sauce or Red Sauce, page 56. Nice for appetizers, or for luncheon with fried rice and a vegetable.

Egg Roll Crepes, page 16
1 dried Oriental mushroom
2 tbs. salad oil
1-1/2 cups fresh mushrooms
3 tbs. diced celery
4 green onions, sliced
1-1/2 cups fresh bean sprouts
1 cup cooked shrimp
2 tbs. cornstarch
1 tsp. salt
1/2 tsp. sugar
2 tsp. soy sauce
1 tbs. flour
2 tbs. water

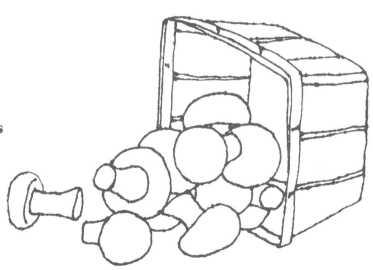

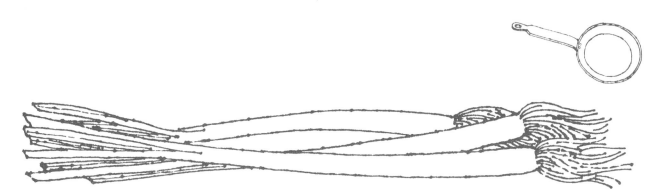

Make crepes as directed. Set aside. Cover dried mushroom with boiling water and let stand 10 minutes. Slice into thin strips. Heat oil in large skillet. Slice fresh mushrooms and saute with celery until mushrooms are limp. Add green onions, bean sprouts and Oriental mushroom strips. Saute 1 to 2 minutes longer. Mix shrimp with cornstarch, salt, sugar and soy sauce. Add to mushroom mixture. Heat 1 to 2 minutes. Set aside. Mix flour and water to make a paste for sealing egg rolls. Place a small amount of filling on the lower third of each egg roll crepe. Bring up bottom flap and start to roll, turning in the sides as you roll. Brush a small amount of the sealing paste along the top of the crepe. Press to seal. Heat oil for deep frying to 375°F. Fry egg rolls two at a time. Turn so all sides brown nicely. Drain on paper toweling. (For appetizers, cut each into 4 pieces.) Serve hot with sauce. Makes 6 to 7 egg rolls.

Mustard Sauce for Egg Roll

1/2 cup mayonnaise
2 tsp. prepared mustard

1/2 tsp. dry mustard
1 tsp. brown sugar

1/2 tsp. lemon juice
1/8 tsp. tumeric

Combine ingredients in small bowl and mix well. Best made a few hours before serving to allow flavors to blend. Makes about 1/2 cup sauce.

Red Sauce for Egg Rolls

2 tbs. cider vinegar
1/4 cup sugar
3 tbs. soy sauce

1/2 cup pineapple juice
2 tbs. currant jelly

1 tbs. cornstarch
2 tbs. water

Combine vinegar, sugar, soy sauce, pineapple juice and currant jelly in small saucepan. Bring to a boil and cook 5 minutes. Dissolve cornstarch in water and add to saucepan. Cook, stirring, until sauce thickens. Makes about 2/3 cup sauce.

BLINI

These tiny pancakes originated in Eastern Europe. Serve them as appetizers with sour cream and caviar, smoked salmon, or sardines.

1 pkg. active dry yeast	1/3 cup sour cream or yogurt
1/2 tsp sugar	1/4 cup buckwheat flour
1/2 tsp. salt	1 cup all-purpose flour
1 cup warm water	1 tbs. melted butter
2 egg yolks	2 egg whites, stiffly beaten

Dissolve yeast, sugar and salt in warm water in mixer bowl. Add egg yolks, sour cream, buckwheat and all-purpose flours. Beat until smooth. Cover bowl with a towel and set in a warm place to rise for 1-1/2 to 2 hours. Mixture will be bubbly. Stir in melted butter. Fold egg whites into mixture just before cooking. Cook blini on a well greased griddle or skillet, or in a 7-place Swedish pancake pan. They should be 3 to 4 inches in diameter. Turn when small holes appear on top. Bake until lightly browned on both sides. Serve immediately. Makes 25 to 30 blini.

CREPE CUPS

Crepes are used instead of pastry to make individual tart shells. Filled with a lovely, light souffle or a favorite quiche filling, they make an attractive presentation for a first course or dessert.

12 Classic Crepes, page 5
butter or no-stick spray shortening
6 5-inch foil tart pans or straight-sided souffle dishes

Make crepes as directed. Butter or spray tart pans (or individual souffle dishes). Place 2 crepes in each tart pan, one on top of the other. Gently form them to the shape of the pan. Spoon desired filling into each crepe cup. Trim edges with kitchen shears so there is just a small amount of crust above the filling. Bake in a 375°F oven the length of time needed for filling to cook. Carefully remove crepe cups from pans to serving dishes, using your fingers to lift them out by the crust edge. Two forks work best for lifting crepe cups out of souffle dishes. Serve immediately. Makes 6 crepe cups.

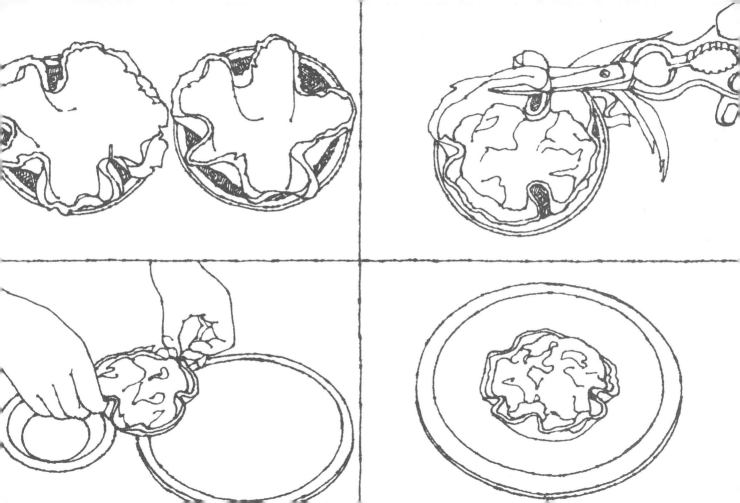

SAVORY CHEESE CREPE CUPS

Serve in place of the cheese course with a glass of red wine.

4 Crepe Cups, page 58	white pepper
2 tbs. butter	1/3 cup crumbled blue, Roquefort or
2 tbs. flour	Gorgonzola cheese
1 cup milk	4 egg whites, stiffly beaten

Make crepe cups as directed and set aside. Melt butter in a small saucepan. Add flour. Cook 2 minutes. Gradually add milk and white pepper. Cook, stirring, until sauce thickens. Remove from heat and stir in cheese. Allow to cool 5 minutes before folding in beaten egg whites. Fill crepe cups with cheese mixture. Trim crepe 1/4 inch above filling with kitchen shears. Bake in 350°F oven about 20 minutes, or until filling is puffed. If crepes brown too quickly, turn oven temperature down. Remove crepe cups to individual serving plates. Serve immediately. Makes 4 crepe cups.

This filling can also be used in 8 crepes folded into triangles, or 8 rolled crepes. Bake until the filling puffs, about 20 minutes.

CLAM SOUFFLE CREPE CUPS

Serve as an appetizer. Use the same filling in rolled crepes, too.

6 Crepe Cups, page 58
3 tbs. butter
2 tbs. minced shallot
1 garlic clove, minced
3 tbs. flour
2 cans (8 ozs. ea.) minced clams

white wine or dry vermouth
2 tbs. chopped pimiento
salt and pepper
2 egg yolks
3 egg whites

Prepare crepe cups as directed and set aside. Melt butter in small saucepan. Add shallot and garlic. Saute 2 minutes. Add flour. Cook 2 minutes. Drain clam juice into measuring cup. Add enough wine to make 1-1/4 cups liquid. Gradually stir into butter-flour mixture. Cook, stirring, until sauce thickens. Stir in clams, pimiento, salt and pepper. Remove from heat. Add a little of the hot mixture to egg yolks and carefully add egg yolks to sauce. Beat whites until stiff peaks form. Fold into clam sauce. Fill crepe cups with souffle mixture. Trim as directed on page 58. Bake in 375°F oven about 25 minutes.

SOUFFLED SALMON CREPE CUPS

Try salmon souffle mixture in rolled crepes, too. It will fill 12. Serve with Cheese Sauce, page 39.

6 Crepe Cups, page 58
1 can (16 ozs.) salmon
3 tbs. butter
3 tbs. flour
1-1/2 cups milk
1 tsp. Worcestershire sauce
2 egg yolks

3 egg whites
2 tbs. chopped pimiento
2 tbs. cilantro leaves, chopped
salt, white pepper
Parmesan cheese
Creamy Mustard Sauce, page 63

Make crepe cups as directed and set aside. Drain and flake salmon, removing skin and bones. Melt butter in small saucepan. Add flour and cook 2 minutes. Gradually add milk and Worcestershire. Cook, stirring, until mixture thickens. Remove from heat. Blend a little of the hot liquid with egg yolks. Add yolks to sauce while stirring vigorously. Add salmon, cilantro, salt and pepper. Beat egg whites until stiff. Fold into salmon mixture. Fill crepe cups and trim.

Sprinkle with Parmesan. Bake in a 375°F oven 20 to 25 minutes or until salmon has puffed. Serve with mustard sauce. Also good with cheese sauce. Makes 6 servings.

Creamy Mustard Sauce

3 tbs. butter
2 tbs. flour
1-1/2 cups half and half
2 tbs. Dijon mustard

2 tsp. Worcestershire sauce
1/8 tsp. white pepper
1/8 tsp. salt
dash nutmeg

Melt butter in small saucepan. Stir in flour and cook 2 minutes. Gradually stir in half and half, mustard, and Worcestershire. Cook, stirring, until sauce thickens. Add pepper, salt and nutmeg. Makes about 1-1/2 cups sauce.

DESSERT CREPES AND CREPE DESSERTS

Crepes for dessert are elegant and appropriate for almost any occasion. Best of all for the busy hostess, they are easy to serve. While they may require some last minute preparation or heating, the crepes, filling and sauce can be made in advance so the final step never takes long. When serving the continental favorite, Crepes Suzette, be sure to allow guests to enjoy the spectacular finish.

This section includes several kinds of crepes and a variety of crepe combinations. Most of the crepes and fillings are interchangeable so enjoy creating different combinations of your own. Keep a supply of crepes in the freezer ready to be thawed and served on short notice. A crepe with a simple jam filling and sprinkled with powdered sugar is pretty and delicious.

Dessert crepes should be approximately 5 inches in diameter. Allow two per serving unless otherwise specified.

CLASSIC DESSERT CREPES

There's no end to the ways dessert crepes can be used. Keep a supply in the freezer!

2 eggs
2 tbs. melted butter
1-1/4 cups milk
2 tbs. brandy or orange liqueur
1 tbs. sugar
1 cup sifted cake flour
1/2 tsp. salt

Place ingredients in blender container in the order listed. Blend at high speed 20 to 30 seconds. Scrape down sides of the container. Blend a few more seconds. Cook according to directions given in the Classic Crepes recipe, page 5. Makes 16 to 20 5-inch crepes.

BANANA CREPES

Fill with Banana Cream Filling on page 75, or fresh fruit and whipped cream.

2 eggs
1-1/4 cups milk
3 tbs. oil
1/2 tsp. vanilla
1 very ripe banana
3 tbs. sugar
1 cup all-purpose flour
1/4 tsp. salt

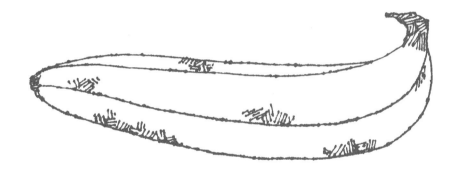

Place ingredients in blender container in the order listed. Cover and blend on high speed 20 to 30 seconds. Scrape sides of container. Blend a few more seconds. Cook according to directions given in the Classic Crepes recipe on page 5. Makes 18 to 22 5-inch crepes.

CHOCOLATE CREPES

Created for chocolate lovers, these are delicious with ice cream!

2 eggs
1 tbs. melted butter
1 sq. (1 oz.) semi-sweet chocolate, melted
1 cup plus 2 tbs. milk
1/2 tsp. vanilla
1/4 cup sugar
1 cup flour
dash of salt and cinnamon

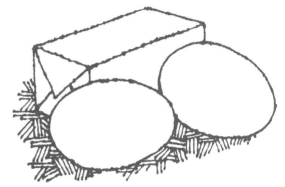

Place ingredients in blender container in order listed. Blend on high speed 20 to 30 seconds. Scrape down the sides of the container. Blend a few more seconds. Cook crepes according to directions given for Classic Crepes recipe on page 5. Makes 18 to 22 5-inch crepes.

GRAHAM DESSERT CREPES

Serve with Honey-Sherry Sauce, page 82; or fill with your favorite fresh fruit combined with yogurt or sour cream.

2 eggs
2 tbs. oil
1-1/3 cups milk
2 tbs. brown sugar or honey
1/2 cup graham flour
1/2 cup all-purpose flour
dash of salt

Place ingredients in blender container in the order listed. Blend on high speed 20 to 30 seconds. Scrape down sides of the container. Blend for a few more seconds. Cook crepes according to directions given for Classic Crepes on page 5. Graham flour has a tendency to settle in the batter, so stir frequently while cooking the crepes. Makes 18 to 22 5-inch crepes.

ORANGE DESSERT CREPES

Use for Crepes Suzette or fill with orange sherbet for a quick dessert.

3 eggs
2 tbs. melted butter
1/4 cup frozen orange juice concentrate, undiluted
1 cup milk
1 tbs. Triple Sec or Cointreau
1 cup flour
2 tbs. sugar
dash salt

Place ingredients in blender container in order listed. Blend at high speed 20 to 30 seconds. Scrape down sides of the container. Blend a few more seconds. Cook according to directions given for Classic Crepes on page 5. Makes 18 to 22 5-inch crepes.

SOUR CREAM DESSERT CREPES

These delicate crepes make a lovely light finish to a meal. Delicious with fresh raspberries and whipped cream, Creamy Lemon Filling, page 85, or Apricot Cream Filling, page 74.

2 eggs
1 cup (1/2 pt.) sour cream
1/3 cup milk
2 tbs. melted butter or oil
1 cup sifted cake flour
2 tbs. sugar
2 tbs. brandy

Place ingredients in blender container in the order listed. Cover and blend on high speed 20 to 30 seconds. Scrape down sides of the container. Blend a few more seconds. Cook according to directions given for Classic Crepes on page 5. Makes 18 to 22 5-inch crepes.

WALNUT DESSERT CREPES

Serve with strawberries or peaches and whipped cream for a perfect summertime dessert.

2 eggs
2 tbs. oil or melted butter
1-1/4 cups milk
1 tbs. honey
1 tbs. cream sherry or brandy
3/4 cup flour
1/2 cup coarsely chopped walnuts
dash of salt

Place ingredients in blender container in the order listed. Blend on high speed 20 to 30 seconds. Scrape down the sides of container. Blend a few more seconds. Cook crepes according to directions given for Classic Crepes on page 5. Makes 18 to 22 5-inch crepes.

APRICOT CREAM CHEESE CREPES

Walnut or graham crepes are good choices for this filling.

8 Walnut or Graham Crepes
1 can (16 ozs.) apricot halves, drained and sliced
3 tbs. apricot brandy or Triple Sec
2 tbs. honey

1 pkg. (3 ozs.) cream cheese
1 tbs. apricot brandy
powdered sugar
whipped cream

Make the crepes of your choice as directed. Set aside. Drain and slice apricots. Marinate in apricot brandy or triple sec and honey for two hours before serving. Soften cream cheese and beat until fluffy with 1 tablespoon apricot brandy. When ready to serve, drain apricot slices. Spread each crepe with a small amount of cream cheese mixture. Place apricots on top of cream cheese. Roll crepes. Place seam side down in buttered, ovenproof serving dish or individual dishes. Sprinkle with powdered sugar. Place under hot broiler 2 to 3 minutes until warmed and lightly browned. Top with whipped cream and serve immediately. Makes 4 servings.

BANANA CREAM CREPES

This banana lover's special makes an ideal late-supper dessert.

12 Banana Crepes, page 67
3 tbs. all-purpose flour
1/3 cup sugar
4 tsp. cornstarch
dash salt
2 cups milk

2 egg yolks
1 tbs. butter
1-1/2 tsp. vanilla
1 large or 2 small bananas, diced
superfine sugar

Make crepes as directed and set aside. Combine flour, sugar, cornstarch and salt in a small saucepan. Add milk gradually. Cook, stirring, over low heat until thickened. Blend a little of the hot mixture into egg yolks. Stir yolks into saucepan. Cook 1 minute. Remove from heat. Add vanilla and butter. Cool. When ready to serve, fold in diced bananas. Place a small amount of filling on each crepe and roll. Place in a buttered, ovenproof serving dish. Sprinkle with superfine sugar. Place under broiler 2 to 3 minutes until slightly warm and the edges are light brown. Serve immediately. Makes 6 servings.

CREAMY CHOCOLATE FILLED CREPES

This is definitely for chocolate lovers. Serve warm or cold.

8 Dessert Crepes, page 66
1 cup milk
1 sq. (1 oz.) bitter chocolate
1/2 sq. (1/2 oz.) semi-sweet chocolate
1/3 cup sugar

2 tsp. cornstarch
1 tbs. dark rum
1 tsp. vanilla
dash salt
1 cup (1/2 pt.) heavy cream, whipped

Make crepes and set aside. Place milk, chocolates, and sugar in small saucepan over low heat until chocolate melts. Dissolve cornstarch in rum and a little water. Add to chocolate mixture. Cook, stirring, until sauce thickens and becomes very smooth. Stir in vanilla and salt. Cool. Spread a small amount of chocolate filling on each crepe. Top with a little whipped cream. Roll up tightly. To serve them slightly warm, place in buttered, ovenproof serving dish. Run under broiler 1 to 2 minutes to heat. Top with more whipped cream and serve immediately. Makes 4 servings.

CHESTNUT RUM CREPES

Chestnut Rum filling in Chocolate Crepes, topped with shavings of chocolate.

12 Chocolate Crepes, page 68
1 cup (1/2 pt.) heavy cream
2 tbs. sugar
1 can (8-3/4 ozs.) sweetened chestnut puree
3 tbs. rum or brandy
chocolate shavings for garnish

Make crepes as directed. Set aside. Whip cream with sugar until stiff peaks form. Stir rum or brandy into chestnut puree. Fold whipped cream into chestnut puree. Fill and roll crepes. Place 2 crepes on each serving plate. Garnish with a dollop of filling and sprinkle with chocolate shavings. Makes 6 servings.

CREPES MELBA

A peaches and cream filling covered with raspberry sauce.

8 Dessert Crepes, page 66
1/2 cup whipping cream
1/4 cup sugar
1/2 cup ricotta cheese
1 cup fresh raspberries
1/4 cup sugar
2 tbs. Triple Sec, Kirsch, or orange juice
2 to 3 fresh peaches, peeled and sliced

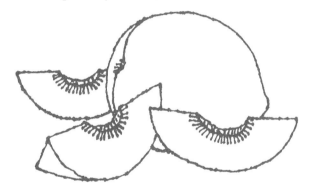

Make crepes as directed. Set aside. Whip cream until soft peaks form. Stir in 1/4 cup sugar and beat until stiff. Fold whipped cream into ricotta cheese. Puree fresh raspberries in blender. Strain to remove seeds. Add 1/4 cup sugar and Triple Sec. Heat sauce just before serving. When ready to fill crepes add peaches to cheese mixture and spoon into crepes. Place filled crepes on serving dishes. Spoon warm raspberry sauce over the crepes. Makes 4 servings.

MINCEMEAT CREPES WITH HARD SAUCE

Mincemeat crepes topped with hard sauce are a holiday favorite.

8 Orange Crepes, page 70   2 cups mincemeat   2 tbs. brandy

Make crepes as directed. Set aside. Heat mincemeat and brandy together in a small saucepan 2 to 3 minutes. Fill crepes with mincemeat mixture. Roll and place seam side up in an ovenproof serving dish. Place under the broiler 2 to 3 minutes to heat and crisp crepes. Top each crepe with a dollop of hard sauce. Makes 4 servings.

Hard Sauce

2 tbs. butter   2 tbs. brandy   2-1/2 to 3 tbs. heavy cream
1 tsp. vanilla   2-1/2 cups powdered sugar

Cream butter, vanilla, brandy and sugar together. Add cream until mixture is the desired consistency. Serve on mincemeat crepes.

CREPES SUZETTE

Prepare and flame this elegant dessert at the table for your guests to see.

12 Orange Crepes, page 70
1/2 cup butter
2 tbs. frozen, undiluted orange juice concentrate
2 tbs. sugar
1 tbs. Triple Sec
grated orange rind from 1 orange

1 tbs. sugar
2 ozs. brandy
1 oz. Triple Sec

Make crepes as directed and set aside. Cream butter in mixer bowl. Gradually beat in orange juice, sugar, Triple Sec and orange rind. Beat until most of the liquid has been absorbed by the butter. When ready to serve the crepes, add the orange butter to a large crepe Suzette pan or skillet over low heat. If cooking at the table, the crepes are stacked on a plate nearby. Pick up one crepe using a fork in one hand and a tablespoon in the other. (In the kitchen without an audience, fingers work well.) Place crepe in the melted orange butter. Quickly turn to coat the other side. Fold in half then fold again. Push to one side of the pan and repeat with another crepe. When all the crepes have been coated and folded, arrange in a single layer in pan, overlapping as necessary. Sprinkle with 1 tablespoon sugar. Combine brandy and Triple Sec and pour over folded crepes. Allow to heat a few seconds. Light with a long match, averting your face and holding hand away from pan. Spoon flaming sauce over crepes and serve as soon as flames die. If preparing crepes in the kitchen, carry flaming pan to the table and serve. Makes 4 generous servings of 3 crepes each.

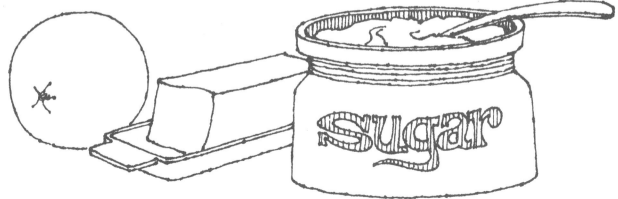

HONEY-SHERRY TRIANGLES

Particularly good with Walnut Crepes, page 72 or Graham Crepes, page 69.

8 crepes
3 tbs. butter
1/2 cup sweet cream sherry
3 tbs. honey
1-1/2 tsp. lemon juice
whipped cream

Make the crepes of your choice. Set aside. Melt butter in small saucepan. Add sherry, honey, lemon juice. Bring to boil. Cook 2 to 3 minutes until mixture thickens slightly and alcohol is boiled off. Dip both sides of crepes in this mixture. Fold into triangles. Place in buttered, ovenproof serving dish or individual serving dishes. Pour remaining sauce over the crepes. Place under broiler until crepes are heated through and lightly browned on edges. Serve with a dollop of whipped cream on each triangle. Makes 4 servings.

JAM OR JELLY CREPES

Here is a quick dessert to satisfy any sweet tooth.

For each Dessert Crepe, page 66, use:

1 to 2 tsp. your favorite jelly, jam, or marmalade
superfine sugar
brandy
whipped cream, slightly sweetened
1 to 2 tsp. chopped nuts

Spread crepe with jelly or jam. Fold in half and fold again, making a triangle. Allow 2 to 3 triangles per person. Place in buttered, ovenproof serving dish, or individual dishes. Sprinkle with sugar and a few drops brandy. Place under broiler to heat and lightly brown. Top with whipped cream and chopped nuts. Serve immediately.

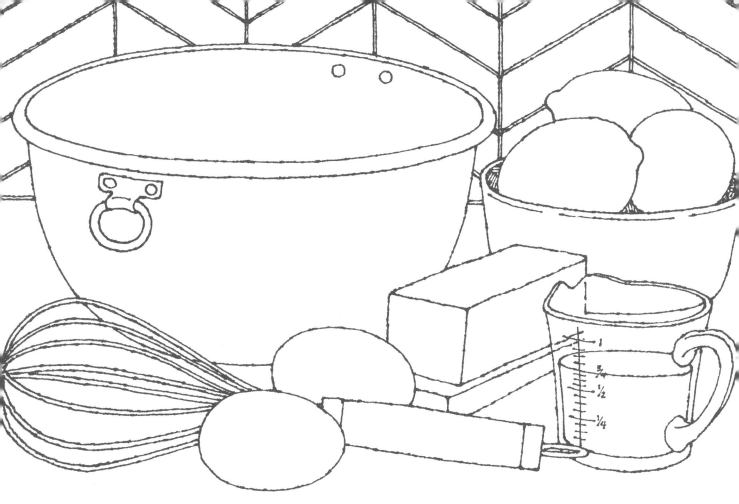

LEMON MERINGUE CREPES

Men are especially fond of lemon crepes with their high meringue topping.

8 Dessert Crepes, page 66
2 eggs, separated
1/2 cup sugar
2 tbs. flour
1/4 cup lemon juice

3/4 cup milk
grated lemon rind
1/8 tsp. lemon extract
2 tbs. sugar

Make crepes as directed. Set aside. Beat egg yolks with 1/2 cup sugar until thick and lemon colored. Add flour and lemon juice. Mix well. Heat milk in small saucepan. Carefully combine with egg yolks. Add lemon rind. Cook, stirring, over low heat until sauce thickens. Remove from heat and add lemon extract. Allow mixture to cool. Just before serving beat egg whites with 2 tablespoons sugar until stiff peaks form. Fill crepes with lemon filling. Roll and place in 4 buttered individual ovenproof serving dishes. Top with meringue. Place in a 450°F oven 5 minutes, or until meringue is lightly browned. Makes 4 servings.

BEIGNETS

Cooked crepes cut into ribbons and fried. Serve hot with Chocolate Rum Sauce, page 87, or Raspberry Sauce, page 87.

1 egg	1 cup all-purpose flour
2 tbs. oil	1/2 tsp. salt
1-1/4 cups milk	1/2 tsp. cinnamon
1 tbs. brandy	1 tbs. sugar

Place egg, oil, milk, brandy, flour and salt in blender container. Blend on high speed 20 to 30 seconds. Scrape down sides of container. Blend a few more seconds. Cook crepes in large 10-inch pan, according to directions given in Classic Crepes recipe, page 5. Cut crepes into 1-inch strips. Heat approximately 1 inch of oil to 375°F in large frying pan or electric skillet. Drop in crepe strips. The strips should stay fairly flat while they are cooking. Turn them over once or twice and remove when they are a nice golden color. Drain for a minute or two on paper toweling. Sprinkle with sugar and cinnamon which have been mixed together. Serve hot. Makes 4 servings.

DIPPING SAUCES FOR BEIGNETS

Serve in individual bowls and dip hot beignets as you eat them.

Raspberry Sauce

1 pkg. (10 ozs.) frozen raspberries, defrosted   1 tsp. lemon juice
1 tbs. Triple Sec or Kirsch

Place berries and syrup in blender container. Cover and puree. Strain through sieve to remove seeds. Stir in liqueur and lemon juice. Makes 1 cup. Also good over crepes, or folded into whipped or sour cream for a filling.

Chocolate Rum Sauce

1 can (5.5 ozs.) Hershey's Chocolate Syrup   1-1/2 tbs. dark rum
1 tsp. vanilla   2 tbs. heavy cream

Combine ingredients in small saucepan. Stir until blended. Heat but do not boil. Makes about 3/4 cup sauce.

CHERRY SAUCE

Spoon this sauce over plain, warm crepes, or serve as a topping for crepes with a vanilla cream or whipped cream filling.

1 can (17 ozs.) pitted dark sweet cherries
2 tbs. sugar
1/8 tsp. lemon extract
2 tsp. cornstarch
2 tbs. water
1 tbs. Kirsch or brandy

Drain juice from cherries into a small saucepan. Set cherries aside. Add sugar and lemon extract to cherry juice. Cook over low heat until sugar dissolves. Mix cornstarch with water and add to juice. Cook, stirring constantly, until sauce boils and thickens. Remove from heat. Add Kirsch and cherries. Serve warm or cold. Makes about 2 cups sauce.

INDEX

omelets omelets
omelets omelets om
omelets omelets
lets omelets ome
omelets omelets o
lets omelets omele
elets omelets om

books designed with giving in mind

Kid's Pets Book	The Compleat American	Working Couples
Make It Ahead	Housewife 1776	Mexican
French Cooking	Low Carbohydrate Cookbook	Sunday Breakfast
Soups & Stews	Kid's Cookbook	Fisherman's Wharf Cookbook
Crepes & Omelets	Italian	Charcoal Cookbook
Microwave Cooking	Cheese Guide & Cookbook	Ice Cream Cookbook
Vegetable Cookbook	Miller's German	Hippo Hamburger
Kid's Arts and Crafts	Quiche & Souffle	Blender Cookbook
Bread Baking	To My Daughter, With Love	The Wok, a Chinese Cookbook
The Crockery Pot Cookbook	Natural Foods	Cast Iron Cookbook
Kid's Garden Book	Chinese Vegetarian	Japanese Country
Classic Greek Cooking	Jewish Gourmet	Fondue Cookbook

from nitty gritty productions

To
Lou Seibert Pappas
teacher, friend, confidante
and
Bob Killough
who never doubted

omelets & crepes

by BOB and COLEEN SIMMONS

Illustrated by MIKE NELSON

Library of Congress Cataloging in Publication Data

Simmons, Bob
    Crepes & Omelets

    Consists of two parts, Crepes & omelets and
Omelets & crepes, inverted with respect to each
other.
    1. Pancakes, waffles, etc. 2. Cookery (Eggs)
I. Simmons, Coleen. II. Title. III. Title:
Omelets & Crepes.
TX770.S56   641.8   76-8426
ISBN 0-911954-35-X

TABLE OF CONTENTS

ALL ABOUT OMELETS

The omelet's reputation for being difficult to make is more rumor than reality. Armed with a few basic techniques, even a beginner can turn out beautiful omelets in a short time. Once the art has been mastered an infinite variety of omelets is possible.

Many ethnic cuisines have omelet-like dishes, but the thrifty, innovative French have elevated the omelet to its present perfection and popularity. It is no surprise that the world's favorite omelet is the classic French rolled omelet.

Omelets are delicious served plain, but it is the addition of fillings and sauces which make the endless variety of omelets possible. We offer a large selection of fillings, and omelets of all descriptions in this book, but the most delicious ones may be those you create yourself! Have fun and use your imagination . . . that's what omelets are all about.

Once you have the basic knowledge of omelet making, there are really only four things needed for a perfect omelet . . . fresh eggs, butter or oil, the right pan, and confidence. The latter will come with practice.

Ingredients

Eggs should be the freshest possible. They can be used right from the refrigerator or at room temperature. (For a puffy omelet, you will find you get better volume if the whites are at room temperature.) All recipes in this book were tested with U.S. Grade A large eggs, which weigh a little over 2 ounces each. If you use eggs of a different size, beat and measure, allowing two fluid ounces for each egg. Also, two fluid ounces of a Second Nature Substitute is equivalent to one large egg.

Fresh, lightly salted butter is best for making omelets. Don't use too much. Vegetable oil with a few drops of dark sesame oil added works well in place of butter. "No-stick" sprays such as Mazola No Stick or Pam are good, especially when using a pan that is not perfectly seasoned. They are also a help for calorie watchers.

White or black pepper is usually used, but we like a few drops of Tabasco sauce instead, because it blends easily throughout the eggs and improves the

2

flavor. If an omelet tastes "hot" after cooking, reduce the amount of Tabasco a bit.

The addition of a teaspoon of water for each egg used, slows the cooking of the eggs and tends to make the finished omelet lighter in texture.

Pans

Omelet pans come in great variety. All will make good omelets if they are properly seasoned before using. The label on a new pan should tell if it has been preseasoned. If the information isn't given, then you should season it. A classic French omelet pan is made of medium weight mild steel, with curved sides about 1-1/2 inches high and a perfectly smooth interior. If the pan is new, the protective coating that may have been applied by the manufacturer must be removed. This is accomplished by scrubbing with kitchen cleanser until the surface is perfectly clean and shiny. Rinse well and dry over low heat. Then, to season it, add one tablespoon vegetable oil and place over low heat until the oil starts to smoke. Distribute oil over the inside of pan with a paper towel and

remove from heat. Before using, heat again and wipe away any excess oil with a paper towel. The pan is now ready to use. Once seasoned, a steel or cast iron pan should be cleaned after use by rubbing with a little coarse salt, instead of being washed. If a pan does require washing it will need to be reseasoned.

If you have a favorite skillet of the correct size, it can be used for omelets if it

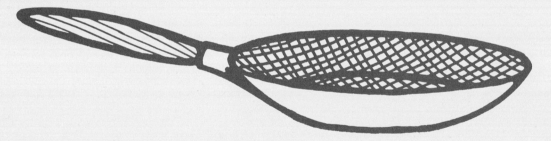

has these characteristics: a smooth inside; is heavy enough to distribute the heat evenly, but light enough to heat quickly; and a handle that can be put into a moderately hot oven since some omelets are finished in the oven. If it has been used for cooking other foods, it must be well seasoned before using for omelets.

Pan Size

Omelet pans vary in size. A pan that measures 7 to 8 inches across the top will produce a 5- to 6-inch omelet and is best for a 2-egg breakfast omelet. For European pans, which are measured in centimeters, this is size 22. Luncheon and supper omelets are usually made with three eggs in a pan that measure 9 to 10 inches, or 26 centimeters, across the top. A 4-egg omelet, just right for a lumberjack or a teenager, is made in a 12-inch or 30-centimeter pan. Rather than make French rolled omelets with more than four eggs, it is better to make several smaller ones.

The first section in this book begins with a basic French rolled omelet recipe with step-by-step directions to demonstrate that omelet making is easy and uncomplicated. Don't be discouraged if your first try doesn't produce a pretty omelet. It will still taste good and the next one will turn out better. Once you master the art of making a perfect omelet, you'll find that nothing is easier, faster or more delicious.

BASIC FRENCH ROLLED OMELET AND FILLINGS

The French rolled omelet is discussed in detail in this section to help omelet makers improve their technique. A well-made omelet is impressive and well worth the effort it takes to perfect this skill.

Omelets are delicious served plain, or varied with fillings and sauces. The fillings offered here are a few of our favorites, but the possibilities are endless. Serve omelets often, they'll never be boring and with a little practice they can be made from start to finish in about three minutes.

Don't overlook omelets when entertaining. They are elegant, quickly made, satisfying and economical. An omelet accompanied by a tossed garden salad, croissants and a glass of wine is sure to please.

FRENCH ROLLED OMELET—A BASIC RECIPE

This recipe is meant to serve as a beginner's guide, and for reference. The "for each egg" formula makes it easy to vary the size of an omelet.

For each egg, use:	2-egg omelet	3-egg omelet
1 tsp. water	2 eggs	3 eggs
dash salt	2 tsp. water	3 tsp. water
1 drop Tabasco	dash salt	dash salt
1-1/2 tsp. butter	2 drops Tabasco	3 drops Tabasco
	1 tbs. butter	1-1/2 tbs. butter

Read the complete recipe and directions carefully before starting to cook.

Gather all ingredients and equipment together before starting to cook.

Prepare filling as directed and set aside until needed.

Break eggs into a small bowl. Add water, salt and Tabasco. Beat with a table fork until whites and yolks are just blended, about 50 strokes or 20 seconds. Eggs should not foam.

8

Put butter into a well seasoned omelet pan or skillet. Place pan over moderately high heat. Rotate pan to distribute butter.

When butter has stopped foaming, but before it has browned, pour eggs into pan.

Allow eggs to set for a few seconds before starting to stir them.

Make circular movements around the bottom of the pan with the flat side of a table fork lifting the cooked egg up as you stir.

When omelet has set on the bottom, tilt the pan and lift the edge of the omelet to allow any uncooked egg on top to flow under cooked portion.

Shake pan vigorously to loosen omelet and prevent it from sticking.

Smooth the top of the omelet with the fork. Cook a few seconds more. An omelet should be only slightly brown on the outside and still creamy, but not liquid on the inside.

Spread about 2 tablespoons filling along the center of the omelet.

Fold omelet into thirds by turning the edge opposite the handle onto the center, covering the filling.

Then fold the edge near the handle over the middle.

Grasp the handle of the pan in your upturned palm. Roll the omelet out onto a warm plate, seam side down.

Brush with melted butter for a nice sheen. Serve immediately.

Avoid having plate too hot as the omelet will continue to cook and toughen. The ideal plate is one that is very warm to the touch but can still be picked up with a bare hand.

As previously noted we will refer to the preceding recipe throughout the book. Individual directions will be given for special recipes where needed. The fillings which follow and those given with the different omelets are for the most part interchangeable. Many of them make delicious crepe fillings, too, so have fun "mixing and matching."

BACON AND AVOCADO FILLING

Ripe avocado and crumbled bits of bacon make a delicious omelet filling.

1/2 ripe avocado
2 slices cooked bacon, crumbled
1 tsp. chopped fresh coriander
1/2 tsp. fresh chives, cut in small pieces
salt and white pepper

Mash avocado and combine with bacon, coriander, a dash of salt and white pepper. Prepare omelets according to directions for Basic Omelet on page 8. Fill with avocado and bacon mixture just before folding. Makes filling for 2 omelets.

BACON, SPINACH AND MUSHROOM FILLING

1 pkg. (10 ozs.) frozen chopped spinach
6 slices bacon
1/4 lb. fresh mushrooms, sliced
5 to 6 green onions, thinly sliced
2 tbs. butter

2 tbs. flour
1-1/4 cups milk
1 tsp. Worcestershire
salt and pepper

Cook spinach according to package directions. Drain and squeeze as dry as possible. Set aside. Cut bacon into small pieces and fry until crisp. Remove bacon and saute fresh mushrooms in bacon fat 4 to 5 minutes. Stir in green onions and cook another minute or two. Drain off excess bacon fat. Melt butter in small saucepan. Add flour. Cook 2 minutes. Gradually add milk, Worcestershire, salt and pepper. Cook, stirring until sauce thickens. Combine spinach, mushrooms and bacon with sauce. Prepare omelets according to Basic Omelet Recipe on page 8. Before folding fill with sauce. Makes filling for 4 omelets.

CREAMED CHICKEN FILLING

Omelets filled with this rich chicken filling make a good luncheon dish for four. Serve with molded cranberry salads or a cranberry relish.

1/4 cup butter or margarine
1/4 cup flour
1-1/2 cups half and half
1 tsp. salt
1/2 tsp. white pepper
2 tbs. sherry
1 tsp. Dijon mustard
2 cups cubed cooked chicken

Melt butter in small saucepan. Stir in flour and cook 2 minutes. Gradually add milk and cook, stirring until sauce thickens. Stir in salt, pepper, sherry, mustard, and cooked chicken. Heat through. Prepare 4 omelets according to directions for Basic Omelet on page 8. Fill with creamed chicken just before folding. Reserve a little of filling for garnish. Makes filling for 4 omelets.

CHICKEN LIVER FILLING

Serve to 3 or 4 guests for luncheon.

2 tbs. butter
1/3 cup onion, chopped
1 cup fresh mushrooms, sliced
1/2 lb. chicken livers
1/2 cup dry sherry

1/2 cup beef bouillon
1 tomato
2 to 3 tbs. sour cream
salt
white pepper

Melt butter in medium sized skillet. Saute onions and mushrooms until soft. Add chicken livers to pan and saute 4 minutes. Remove onions, mushrooms and chicken livers and set aside. Turn heat to high. Pour in sherry and beef bouillon. Reduce mixture to half. Return onions, mushrooms, and chicken livers to pan. Peel, seed, and chop tomato. Add to pan. Heat through. Remove from heat and stir in sour cream. Adjust seasoning. Prepare omelets according to directions for Basic Omelet on page 8. Fill with chicken livers before folding. Reserve a little of the filling for garnish. Makes filling for 3 to 4 omelets.

DRIED BEEF FILLING

1 jar (2-1/2 ozs.) dried beef
1 cup hot water
3 tbs. butter
3 tbs. flour
2 cups milk

1 tsp. Worcestershire sauce
1 tsp. prepared mustard
white pepper
chopped parsley

Place dried beef in small bowl. Cover with hot water and let stand 2 minutes to remove excess salt. Drain well. cut into strips with kitchen scissors. Melt butter in small saucepan. Briefly saute beef strips in butter. Add flour and cook 2 minutes. Gradually stir in milk, Worcestershire, mustard and white pepper. Cook, stirring, until sauce thickens. Prepare omelets according to directions for Basic Omelet on page 8. Fill omelet with sauce, reserving a little of the sauce to garnish top. Sprinkle with chopped parsley. Makes filling and sauce for 3 omelets.

SLOPPY JOE FILLING

3/4 lb. lean ground beef
1 small onion, chopped
1 small clove garlic, minced
1 tbs. chili powder
1 can (10-1/2 ozs.) beef consomme

1 tbs. Worcestershire sauce
1/4 tsp. dry mustard
3 tbs. tomato puree or catsup
few grains cayenne pepper
salt

Saute beef in medium sized skillet until it browns. Crumble it as it cooks. Remove beef from pan. Pour off all but 2 tablspoons of the pan drippings. Saute onion and garlic in drippings until soft and transparent. Add chili powder and mix well. Return beef to pan. Stir in consomme, Worcestershire, dry mustard, tomato puree, and cayenne pepper. Simmer uncovered for approximately 30 minutes until most of moisture has evaporated. Season to taste, adding more cayenne or chili powder if desired. Prepare omelets according to directions for Basic Omelet, page 8. Fill with meat mixture before folding. Makes filling for 4 to 5 omelets.

JOE'S SPECIAL FILLING

Hamburger, mushrooms, and spinach make another version of a Bay Area favorite.

2 tbs. butter
1/2 lb. fresh mushrooms, sliced
1/2 lb. hamburger
1/2 cup onion, chopped
salt and pepper
4 cups coarsely chopped raw spinach, or
     1 cup cooked, drained, chopped spinach
1 can (10-1/2 ozs.) Franco American Beef Gravy
2 tbs. Madeira or brandy

Heat butter in large skillet. When foaming, saute mushrooms 3 to 4 minutes. Remove from pan and set aside. In same skillet saute hamburger and onion. Crumble hamburger with spatula as it is cooking. When hamburger is done drain off excess grease. Add half of the sauteed mushrooms to hamburger and stir in

18

spinach. Heat beef gravy in small saucepan. Add Madeira and boil vigorously 3 to 5 minutes until sauce is reduced slightly. Add half of the sauce to meat mixture and the rest to the mushrooms. Prepare 4 omelets according to directions for Basic Omelet, page 8. Divide the hamburger filling into four parts. Fill each omelet with one-quarter of filling before folding. Top each omelet with the mushroom gravy sauce. Makes filling and sauce for 4 omelets.

19

SAUSAGE AND PEPPERS FILLING

4 to 6 small brown and serve sausages
1/2 large green pepper, diced
1/2 large red pepper, diced
1/2 medium onion, coarsely chopped
1/4 cup white wine or sherry
salt and pepper

Brown sausages in medium sized skillet. Drain on paper toweling. Cut into 1/2-inch pieces and set aside. Drain all but a little of the fat from skillet. Add the peppers and onion. Saute until soft but not brown, adding a little butter if necessary. Add sausages and wine. Turn up heat and cook 2 to 3 minutes until most of the liquid has evaporated. Prepare 2 omelets according to directions for Basic Omelet on page 8. Fill with peppers and sausages before folding. Makes filling for 2 omelets.

SALAMI AND ONION RING FILLING

Onion rings give this omelet a nice crunchy texture.

4 eggs
4 drops Tabasco
salt
2 tbs. chopped parsley
6 thin slices salami, diced
1/4 cup canned onion rings

Beat eggs with Tabasco, salt, parsley and salami. Divide egg mixture to make two omelets. Prepare omelets according to directions for Basic Omelet on page 8. Just before folding, sprinkle each with half of the onion rings. Makes 2 omelets.

ANCHOVY CROUTON AND CHEESE FILLING

Crunchy croutons and cheese make an interesting omelet filling.

1 tbs. butter
1 tbs. cream cheese
2 anchovy fillets, washed, dried and finely chopped
1/2 tsp. brandy
2 slices bread
Parmesan cheese

Combine butter, cream cheese, anchovies and brandy. Mix to a smooth paste. Toast bread lightly in toaster. Remove crusts. Spread with anchovy mixture. Sprinkle with Parmesan cheese. Place in 350°F oven about 10 minutes until topping is lightly browned. Cut into 1/2-inch croutons. Prepare omelets according to directions given for Basic Omelet on page 8. Before folding fill each with 2 tablespoons croutons and 2 tablespoons Parmesan or other mild cheese. Makes filling for 4 omelets.

SARDINE AND CAPER FILLING

1 can (4-3/8 ozs.) skinless sardines packed in oil
1-1/2 tbs. butter
1 tbs. flour
3/4 cup light cream
1 tbs. Dijon mustard
1 tsp. Worcestershire sauce
1/8 tsp. white pepper
1/4 tsp. salt
nutmeg
1 tbs. capers, drained

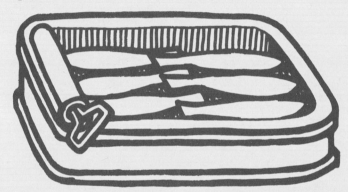

   Drain oil from sardines. Flake three sardines for the sauce and leave the rest whole. Melt butter in a small saucepan. Add flour. Cook 2 minutes. Gradually stir in cream, mustard, Worcestershire, pepper, salt, nutmeg and capers. Cook, stirring until sauce thickens. Stir in flaked sardines. Prepare 2 omelets according to directions for Basic Omelet, page 8. Before folding fill each with two sardines. Fold and top with sauce. Makes filling and sauce for 2 omelets.

23

NEW ORLEANS FILLING

Shrimp Creole makes a delicious omelet filling. Use small or medium sized shrimp.

2 tbs. butter
1 cup finely chopped onion
1/2 cup finely chopped green pepper
1/3 cup finely sliced celery
1/2 clove garlic, crushed
1/3 cup vermouth
2 medium tomatoes

1/2 tsp. thyme
1 bay leaf
1 tsp. Worcestershire sauce
4 drops Tabasco
dash cayenne pepper
2/3 lb. shelled, deveined shrimp

Melt butter in large skillet. Saute onion, green pepper, celery and garlic together. When almost soft, add vermouth. Peel, seed and chop tomatoes. Add tomatoes and seasonings to pan. Cook over fairly high heat for about 10 minutes. Add shrimp. Lower heat and cook until shrimp turns pink. Prepare omelets as directed in Basic Omelet recipe, page 8. Fill with shrimp mixture just before folding. Makes fillings for 4 omelets.

24

CURRIED SHRIMP FILLING

2 tbs. butter
2 tbs. flour
1/2 tsp. curry powder
1-1/4 cups milk
1/4 tsp. celery salt
white pepper
1/2 lb. small cooked shrimp

Melt butter in small saucepan. Stir in flour and curry powder. Cook 2 minutes. Gradually add milk, celery salt and pepper. Cook until sauce thickens. Stir in cooked shrimp and heat through. Prepare omelets according to directions for Basic Omelet on page 8. Use part of the shrimp mixture for filling, reserving some for garnish. Makes filling for 2 to 3 omelets.

Variation: Cook 1/2 pound scallops in 2 tablespoons butter and use instead of the shrimp.

SOLE AND BEAN SPROUT FILLING

2 tbs. vegetable oil
1/2 tsp. sesame oil
1/2 cup sliced fresh mushrooms
3 green onions, thinly sliced
1/2 lb. filet of sole
1/4 lb. fresh bean sprouts

1 tsp. fresh ginger, minced (optional)
1/2 cup chicken stock
2 tbs. dry sherry
1 tsp. cornstarch
1 tbs. soy sauce
salt and white pepper

Heat vegetable oil and sesame oil in medium sized skillet. Saute mushrooms and onions 3 to 4 minutes. Remove from pan and set aside. Slice fish into strips 3/4-inch wide and 2 inches long. Flour lightly. Saute in same pan over high heat for a minute on each side. Add bean sprouts and ginger. Return mushrooms and onion to pan. Toss lightly. Add chicken stock and sherry. Cook over high heat to reduce slightly. Dissolve cornstarch in soy sauce. Stir into pan juices to thicken. Season to taste. Prepare omelets according to directions for Basic Omelet, page 8. Fill with fish mixture before folding. Serve immediately. Makes filling for 2 omelets.

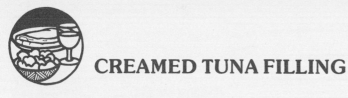

CREAMED TUNA FILLING

Good for French rolled omelets or for the Baked Omelet Roll, page 62.

3 tbs. butter
3 tbs. flour
1-1/2 cups milk
1/2 tsp. celery salt
white pepper
1 can (6-1/2 ozs.) tuna, drained
2 tbs. capers, drained
1/2 cup sliced green olives

Melt butter in small saucepan. Add flour and cook 2 minutes. Gradually add milk. Cook, stirring over low heat until sauce thickens. Stir in celery salt, white pepper, tuna, capers and olives. Heat through.

ASPARAGUS FILLING

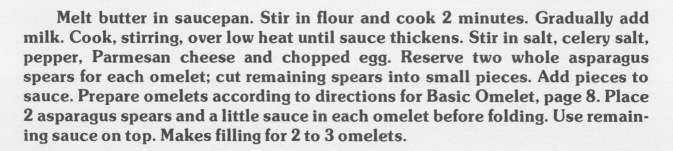

2 tbs. butter
2 tbs. flour
1 cup milk
1/2 tsp. each salt and celery salt
1/4 tsp. white pepper
1/4 cup grated Parmesan cheese
1 hard-cooked egg, chopped
10 asparagus spears

Melt butter in saucepan. Stir in flour and cook 2 minutes. Gradually add milk. Cook, stirring, over low heat until sauce thickens. Stir in salt, celery salt, pepper, Parmesan cheese and chopped egg. Reserve two whole asparagus spears for each omelet; cut remaining spears into small pieces. Add pieces to sauce. Prepare omelets according to directions for Basic Omelet, page 8. Place 2 asparagus spears and a little sauce in each omelet before folding. Use remaining sauce on top. Makes filling for 2 to 3 omelets.

CREAMED CAULIFLOWER AND CHEESE FILLING

1 tbs. butter
1 tbs. flour
1 cup milk
2 to 3 drops Tabasco
1/2 cup grated sharp cheese
1-1/2 cups cooked cauliflower, cut into small pieces
salt and pepper

Melt butter in small saucepan. Add flour. Cook 2 minutes. Gradually add milk and Tabasco. Cook, stirring until sauce thickens. Stir in cheese and cauliflower. Season to taste. Cook another minute or two until filling is heated. Prepare omelets according to directions for Basic Omelet on page 8. Before folding fill with cauliflower and cheese sauce. Reserve a little of the mixture for topping. Sprinkle very lightly with paprika. Makes filling for 3 omelets.

EGGPLANT AND TOMATO FILLING

2 cups eggplant, peeled and diced in 1/2-inch pieces
1 tsp. salt
3 tomatoes
1/2 tsp. sweet basil
pepper
2 tbs. butter
oil for frying

Cut eggplant into 1/2-inch dice. Put into a strainer. Sprinkle with salt and let stand 20 minutes. Peel, seed and chop tomatoes. Combine tomatoes, basil and pepper. Heat butter in a medium skillet. Add tomatoes and cook 10 to 15 minutes until tomatoes are soft and have formed a thick sauce. Rinse eggplant well to remove salt. Pat dry. Heat 1/4-inch vegetable oil in medium skillet. When quite hot add eggplant and cook 5 to 10 minutes until eggplant is crisp and lightly browned. Prepare omelets according to directions for Basic Omelet, page 8. Before folding omelets fill with sauteed eggplant. Fold and top with tomato sauce. Makes filling and sauce for 3 omelets.

SHERRY MUSHROOM FILLING

Sherry flavored mushrooms with sour cream make an excellent omelet filling.

1/4 lb. fresh mushrooms, sliced
1 bunch green onions, sliced
2 to 3 tbs. butter
1/4 cup sherry or brandy
1 tsp. Bovril
1/2 cup sour cream
dash nutmeg
salt and pepper

Saute sliced mushrooms and onions in butter until soft. Add sherry or brandy and saute until most of liquid has evaporated. Stir in Bovril, sour cream, nutmeg, salt and pepper. Heat through. Do not boil. Prepare omelets according to directions for Basic Omelet on page 8. Fill with mushrooms just before folding. Makes filling for 2 to 3 omelets.

THREE MUSHROOM FILLING

4 dried black Oriental mushrooms
1 cup boiling water
1/4 lb. fresh mushrooms, sliced
3 thinly sliced green onions
2 tbs. vegetable oil
2 tbs. dry sherry
1/2 tsp. lemon juice

1 can (10-1/2 ozs.) beef bouillon
2 tsp. soy sauce
1 tbs. cornstarch
2 tbs. water
1/8 tsp. white pepper
1 can (4 ozs.) button mushrooms

Cover dried mushrooms with boiling water. Let stand for 20 minutes. Squeeze dry. Remove stems and cut mushrooms into 1/4-inch by 1-inch strips. Saute fresh mushrooms and green onions in oil over high heat 4 to 5 minutes. Add black mushrooms, sherry, lemon juice, bouillon, and soy sauce to skillet. Cook over medium high heat 8 to 10 minutes to reduce the sauce slightly. Dissolve cornstarch in water. Add pepper and drained button mushrooms to the pan. Over low heat slowly add cornstarch to the sauce, stirring constantly, until it becomes the consistency of heavy cream. It may not be necessary to add all of the cornstarch. Makes filling for 4 omelets.

ONION AND GREEN PEPPER FILLING

1 medium onion, thinly sliced
1 medium green pepper, thinly sliced
2 tbs. butter
salt and pepper
3 tbs. grated Swiss or Parmesan cheese

Saute the onion and green pepper slices very slowly in butter. They should be soft but not brown. Season with salt and pepper. If you make this ahead, reheat just before filling omelets. Prepare 3 omelets according to Basic Omelet recipe on page 8. Fill each omelet with the onion and pepper mixture and sprinkle a tablespoon of cheese on each before folding. Makes filling for 3 omelets.

CREAMED PEAS AND MUSHROOM FILLING

1 pkg. (10 ozs.) frozen peas
2 tbs. butter
8 to 10 fresh mushrooms, sliced
3 green onions, sliced
3 tbs. butter
3 tbs. flour
1-3/4 cups milk
1/2 tsp. celery salt
salt and pepper

Cook frozen peas according to package directions. Drain and set aside. Melt 2 tablespoons butter in a skillet. Saute mushrooms over high heat 4 to 5 minutes. Add green onions and cook another minute or two. Set aside. Melt butter in small saucepan. Stir in flour. Cook 2 minutes. Gradually add milk and celery salt. Cook, stirring until sauce thickens. Add peas and mushrooms to sauce. Adjust seasoning. Use as filling for Basic Omelet, page 8, or for Baked Omelet Roll, page 62. Makes 4 servings.

SPANISH FILLING

2 tbs. olive oil
1/2 cup chopped onion
1/2 cup chopped green pepper
1 medium tomato
2 tbs. diced pimiento or red pepper
2 tbs. diced ham
salt and pepper

Heat olive oil in skillet. Saute onion and green pepper until soft. Peel, seed and chop tomato. Add tomato, pimiento, ham, salt and pepper to skillet. Cook until mixture is fairly dry. Prepare omelets according to Basic Omelet recipe on page 8. Fill omelet before folding. Makes filling for 2 omelets.

TOMATO, MUSHROOM, AND BACON FILLING

1 ripe tomato
2 tbs. butter
4 large mushrooms, sliced
2 pieces cooked bacon, crumbled
salt and pepper

Peel, seed, coarsely chop tomato. Melt 1 tablespoon butter in small saucepan and cook tomato until soft and fairly dry. Saute mushrooms in 1 tablespoon butter. When limp add to tomatoes with crumbled bacon, salt and pepper. Simmer 3 to 4 minutes to blend flavors. Makes fillings for 2 omelets.

ZUCCHINI AND TOMATO FILLING

2 cups (about 2 medium) zucchini, sliced
2 tomatoes
1 cup onion, finely chopped
2 tbs. olive oil
1 tsp. salt
1 tsp. Italian herb seasoning
1/2 tsp. black pepper
Parmesan cheese

Cut zucchini in half lengthwise and slice thinly. Peel, seed, and coarsely chop tomatoes. Saute onion in olive oil until soft and translucent. Add sliced zucchini. Stir until zucchini is well coated with oil. Add tomatoes, salt, Italian herb seasoning and pepper. Saute over medium heat until zucchini is tender and tomato juices have been absorbed. Mixture should be quite dry. Prepare omelets according to Basic Omelet recipe on page 8. Just before folding fill with zucchini mixture. Sprinkle with Parmesan cheese. Makes filling for 4 omelets.

ROLLED FILLED OMELETS AND FRITTATA

A rolled filled omelet is a simple variation of the classic French omelet. The technique is the same, but instead of a filling being rolled up in the omelet, the filling ingredients are sauteed with the butter in the omelet pan. Then the beaten eggs are poured over and everything becomes mixed as the omelet is stirred. It is rolled and served in the same way as the French omelet.

When making frittata, the Italian word for omelet, all ingredients including the eggs are mixed together and poured into heated oil. When partially set, the frittata is placed under the broiler to finish. It is good served warm or at room temperature and makes an excellent appetizer.

ASPARAGUS AND LEMON CRUMB OMELET

Make this omelet for luncheon when fresh asparagus is in season.

For each omelet

3 eggs
3 drops Tabasco
1 tbs. water
dash salt

3/4 cup cooked asparagus
2 tbs. butter
2 tbs. fresh bread crumbs, grated
grated rind of 1/2 lemon

Beat eggs, Tabasco, water and salt with a fork in a small bowl until well combined. Set aside. Cut asparagus into 1-inch pieces. Melt butter in a 10-inch omelet pan or a very well seasoned skillet. When foaming add bread crumbs and cook over low heat until they start to color. Add asparagus and lemon rind. Continue to cook until crumbs are golden brown. Crumbs will turn brown very rapidly once they start coloring. Pour egg mixture on top of asparagus mixture. Prepare omelet according to directions for Basic Omelet, page 8. Serve on a warm plate.

BROCCOLI AND PROSCUITTO OMELET

The filling and eggs are cooked together in this rolled omelet.

For each omelet

3 eggs	1-1/2 tbs. butter
3 drops Tabasco	1/3 cup cooked broccoli, thinly sliced
1 tbs. water	1 tbs. proscuitto or country ham, diced
dash salt	2 green onions, thinly sliced

Beat eggs, Tabasco, water, and salt with a fork in a small bowl until well combined. Set aside. Melt butter in a 10-inch omelet pan or a very well seasoned skillet. When foaming add broccoli, proscuitto, and green onions. Cook over low heat 2 to 3 minutes until butter is lightly browned. Pour egg mixture into skillet on top of broccoli. Prepare omelet according to directions for Basic Omelet, page 8. Serve on a warm plate.

CRAB AND AVOCADO OMELET

A good choice for a special luncheon. Accompany with a green salad and a glass of white wine.

For each omelet

3 eggs	1-1/2 tbs. butter
3 drops Tabasco	2/3 cup flaked crab meat
1 tbs. water	2 green onions, thinly sliced
dash salt	1/2 cup diced avocado

Beat eggs, Tabasco, water and salt with a fork in a small bowl until well combined. Set aside. Melt butter in a 10-inch omelet pan or a well seasoned skillet. When foaming add crab and green onions. Cook 2 to 3 minutes until butter is lightly browned. Pour egg mixture into skillet on top of crab meat. Sprinkle with diced avocado. Prepare omelet according to directions for Basic Omelet, page 8. Serve on a warm plate.

SHRIMP AND WALNUT OMELET

For each omelet

3 eggs
3 drops Tabasco
1 tbs. water
dash salt
1-1/2 tbs. butter

3 to 4 drops sesame oil
1/2 cup small cooked shrimp
1 green onion, thinly sliced
3 tbs. coarsely chopped walnuts

Beat eggs, Tabasco, water and salt with a fork in a small bowl until well combined. Set aside. Heat butter and oil in a 10-inch omelet pan or a well seasoned skillet. When foaming add shrimp, onion, and walnuts. Cook 2 to 3 minutes over low heat until butter is lightly browned. Pour egg mixture into skillet on top of shrimp. Cook and finish omelet according to directions for Basic Omelet, page 8. Serve on a warm plate.

SAUTEED SCALLOPS OMELET

Scallops, parsley and garlic are cooked with the eggs in this omelet.

For each omelet

3 eggs	flour
3 drops Tabasco	1/2 cup scallops, cut in 1/4-inch slices
1 tbs. water	1/4 tsp. minced garlic
dash salt	1 tsp. minced parsley
1-1/2 tbs. butter	

Beat eggs, Tabasco, water and salt with a fork in a small bowl until well combined. Set aside. Melt butter in a 10-inch omelet pan or a well seasoned skillet. Lightly flour scallop pieces. Shake off excess flour. Add scallops and garlic to foaming butter. Cook 3 to 4 minutes over low heat until scallops are lightly browned. Pour egg mixture into skillet on top of scallops. Add parsley. Cook and finish omelet according to directions for Basic Omelet, page 8. Serve on a warm plate.

GREEN BEAN OMELET

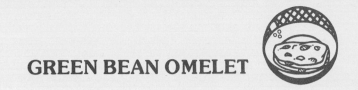

For each omelet

3 eggs
3 drops Tabasco
1 tbs. water
dash salt
1-1/2 tbs. butter
1/2 cup cooked green beans, cut into 1-inch pieces
2 tbs. cooked crumbled bacon or 1 tbs. bacon bits
2 green onions, very thinly sliced

Beat eggs, Tabasco, water, and salt with a fork in a small bowl until well combined. Set aside. Melt butter in a 10-inch omelet pan or a well seasoned skillet. When foaming add green beans, bacon and green onions. Cook over low heat until butter is lightly browned. Pour egg mixture into skillet on top of green beans. Prepare omelet according to directions for Basic Omelet, page 8. Serve on a warm plate.

MUSHROOM OMELET

A quick mushroom omelet with the filling and eggs cooked together

For each omelet

3 eggs
3 drops Tabasco
1 tbs. water
dash salt
1-1/2 tbs. butter
4 fresh mushrooms, sliced
2 green onions sliced.

Beat eggs, Tabasco, water and salt with a fork in a small bowl until well combined. Set aside. Melt butter in a 10-inch omelet pan or a well seasoned skillet. When foaming add mushrooms and green onions. Cook over medium heat 4 to 5 minutes. Pour egg mixture into skillet on top of mushrooms. Cook and finish omelet according to directions for Basic Omelet, page 8. Serve on a warm plate.

NOODLE OMELET

Cooked noodles add an unusual texture to this omelet.

For each omelet

3 eggs	2/3 cup cooked noodles, cut into 1-inch pieces
3 drops Tabasco	1/4 cup flaked tuna
1 tbs. water	2 to 3 stuffed green olives, thinly sliced
dash salt	1-2 cup grated sharp cheese
2 tbs. butter	

Beat eggs, Tabasco, water, and salt with a fork in a small bowl until well combined. Set aside. Melt butter in a 10-inch omelet pan or a well seasoned skillet. When foaming add noodles, tuna and olives. Cook over medium heat 2 to 3 minutes until butter and noodles are very lightly browned. Pour egg mixture into skillet on top of noodles. Sprinkle with grated cheese. Cook and finish omelet according to directions for Basic Omelet, page 8. Serve on a warm plate.

49

ZUCCHINI FRITTATA

This makes good lunch box or picnic fare.

2 cups grated zucchini
salt
2 tomatoes
2 tbs. olive oil

4 eggs
5 green onions, sliced
1/2 cup Parmesan cheese
1 tsp. sweet basil

1 tsp. Dijon mustard
1/2 tsp. salt
pepper to taste
dash of nutmeg

Grate zucchini coarsely. Sprinkle with salt and let stand 15 to 20 minutes. Rinse zucchini and squeeze as dry as possible. Peel, seed and chop tomatoes. Heat olive oil in a 7- or 8-inch ovenproof skillet. Combine zucchini and remaining ingredients. Mix well and pour into heated pan. Cook over low heat until eggs begin to set. Lift around the sides of pan so the uncooked portion flows under the cooked part. When partially set, place under broiler as far away from heat as possible for 5 to 10 minutes, or until top is set and lightly browned. Slide out of pan onto a plate lined with paper toweling. Let drain. Cut into wedges. Serve warm or at room temperature. Makes 2 to 3 servings.

GARBANZO BEAN FRITTATA

2 tbs. olive oil
1 small onion, chopped
1/4 cup chopped pimiento
1/4 cup sliced ripe olives
1 cup cooked garbanzo beans
2 tbs. chopped parsley

1/2 tsp. sweet basil
4 eggs
salt and pepper
1 tbs. olive oil
Parmesan cheese for topping

Heat olive oil in a 7- to 8-inch ovenproof skillet. Saute onions until soft. Place onions in small mixing bowl. Combine with pimiento, olives, garbanzo beans, parsley, basil, eggs, salt and pepper. Mix well. Add 1 tablespoon olive oil to oil remaining in skillet. Pour in egg mixture. Cook until eggs start to set. Lift around sides of pan so the uncooked portion flows under the cooked part. When partially set, top with Parmesan cheese. Place under broiler as far away from heat as possible for 5 to 10 minutes, or until top is set and lightly browned. Slide out of pan onto a plate lined with paper toweling. Let drain. Cut into wedges. Serve warm or at room temperature. Makes 2 to 3 servings.

GREEN BEAN FRITTATA

4 eggs
5 to 6 green onions, thinly sliced
1-1/2 cups cooked green beans, cut into 1-inch pieces
1 cup Parmesan cheese
1 small clove garlic, crushed
1/4 tsp. oregano
3 tbs. fresh parsley, chopped
salt and pepper
3 tbs. olive oil

Combine all the ingredients except oil in a mixing bowl. Mix well. Heat oil in a 7- to 8-inch ovenproof skillet. Pour in egg mixture. Cook until eggs start to set. Lift around sides of pan so the uncooked portion flows under the cooked part. When partially set, place under broiler as far away from heat as possible for 5 to 10 minutes, or until top is set and lightly browned. Slide out of pan onto a plate lined with paper toweling. Let drain. Cut into wedges. Serve warm or at room temperature. Makes 2 to 3 servings.

FRITTATA PROVENCALE

The filling from the Provencale Omelet Sandwich is used to make this frittata.

1-1/2 to 2 cups Provencale filling, page 70
4 eggs
salt and pepper
1/2 cup sharp cheese, grated
2 tbs. olive oil

Combine Provencale filling with eggs, salt, pepper and cheese. Mix well. Heat oil in a 7- to 8-inch ovenproof skillet. Pour egg mixture into heated pan. Cook until eggs start to set. Lift around the sides of pan so uncooked portion flows under the cooked part. When partially set, place under broiler as far away from heat as possible for 5 to 10 minutes, or until top is set and lightly browned. Slide out of pan onto a plate lined with paper toweling. Let drain. Cut into wedges. Serve warm or at room temperature. Makes 2 to 3 servings.

SPINACH FRITTATA

1 pkg. (10 ozs.) frozen chopped spinach
4 egg yolks
5 to 6 green onions, thinly sliced
1 tbs. Dijon mustard
salt and pepper
1 tbs. chopped parsley

1 tsp. sweet basil
dash nutmeg
1/3 cup Parmesan cheese
4 egg whites
3 tbs. olive oil
Parmesan cheese

Cook spinach as directed on package. Drain and squeeze as dry as possible. Combine spinach, egg yolks, seasonings and Parmesan cheese. Mix well. Beat egg whites until stiff peaks form. Fold into spinach mixture. Heat olive oil in a 7- to 8-inch ovenproof skillet. Pour in egg mixture. Cook over low heat until eggs start to set. Lift around sides of pan so the uncooked portion flows under the cooked part. Sprinkle with Parmesan cheese. When partially set place under broiler as far away from heat as possible for 5 to 10 minutes, or until top is set and lightly browned. Slide out of pan onto a plate lined with paper toweling. Let drain. Cut into wedges. Serve warm or at room temperature. Makes 2 to 3 servings.

MORE OMELETS
PLAIN AND FANCY

This section could be called a potpourri of omelet recipes. Some are for old favorites, such as puffy omelets, while some of the others offer unusual ideas for serving plain omelets.

Puffy omelets with their souffle-like consistency are as pretty as they are delicious. Usually served with a filling and a sauce, they make marvelous luncheon and late-supper entrees. Their lovely texture is achieved by separating the eggs and folding the stiffly beaten whites into the yolks, which have been combined with the seasonings and other ingredients. Puffy omelets are started over direct heat then finished in a hot oven. One omelet usually makes two or more servings.

Especially for those who can't eat eggs we have included an excellent recipe for an omelet using Second Nature Egg Substitute.

PUFFY OMELET

Serve plain or with a filling. Save a little filling to spoon over the top.

For each omelet:

2 eggs whites
2 drops Tabasco
dash salt
2 eggs yolks
2 tsp. cold water
1 tbs. butter

Add salt and Tabasco to egg whites. Beat until stiff peaks form. Blend egg yolks and water. Fold into egg whites. Heat butter in a 7- to 8-inch ovenproof omelet pan. When foamy add egg mixture to pan and allow to set on the bottom for a few seconds. Place under broiler until top is lightly browned. Spread half of omelet with filling. Save a little for the top. Fold omelet in half. Serve immediately on warm plate. Makes one omelet.

THIN OMELETS

Use thin omelets to make the Bacon and Tomato Breakfast Sandwich, page 66, or with Pesto Omelet Filling, page 60, to make a layered omelet.

5 eggs	salt
3 tbs. cream	3 tbs. butter
4 drops Tabasco	

Beat eggs with cream, Tabasco and salt. Melt 1/2 teaspoon butter in 7- to 8-inch omelet pan. Pour egg mixture into measuring cup. Use one-fourth of mixture for each omelet. When butter is foaming pour in one part of egg mixture. Stir center with fork and lift eggs around edges so uncooked part can flow under the cooked eggs. Turn out on a plate and add another 1/2 teaspoon butter to pan. When foamy, add one-fourth of mixture. Continue until you have cooked four omelets.

Note: This recipe will also make 5 thinner omelets if you divide egg mixture into 5 parts.

PESTO FILLING FOR A LAYERED OMELET

Pesto filling is alternated with tomatoes and ham between thin omelet layers, page 59, and then cut in pie-shaped wedges.

2 tbs. olive oil
1 tbs. lemon juice
1/4 cup parsley sprigs
1 cup fresh basil leaves
1 small clove garlic, mashed
1/2 tsp. each salt and sugar
1/4 cup pine nuts, or slivered almonds
1/4 cup Parmesan cheese
1 cup chopped tomato pieces
1 cup slivered ham pieces or bacon pieces

Place olive oil, lemon juice, parsley, basil, garlic, salt, sugar, nuts in blender container. Puree until fairly smooth. Stir in the cheese. Prepare 5 Thin Egg Omelets according to directions on page 59. Leave flat. Spread the first cooked

omelet with one-half of the pesto filling. Place another cooked omelet directly on top of the first. Spread it with tomatoes. Top with another omelet and cover it with the ham or bacon. The next omelet should be spread with the remaining pesto filling. Top with the last omelet. Sprinkle with Parmesan cheese. Place in 350°F oven 12 to 15 minutes to heat through. Cut into wedges to serve. Makes 4 to 5 servings.

Note: Substitute chopped walnuts for pine nuts or almonds.

Use Pesto filling in French rolled omelet omitting the tomatoes and ham.

BAKED OMELET ROLL

Fill with Creamed Peas and Mushrooms, page 36; Creamed Tuna Filling, page 28; or Provencale Omelet Filling, page 70.

2 tbs. butter
2 tbs. flour
1 cup milk
1/2 tsp. salt
white pepper
4 eggs, separated
4 drops Tabasco

Melt butter in a small saucepan. Stir in flour. Cook 2 minutes. Gradually add milk. Cook over low heat until sauce thickens. Add salt and pepper. Beat egg yolks with Tabasco. Carefully combine egg yolks with a little of the hot mixture, and add them to the sauce. Beat egg whites until stiff. Fold into sauce. Butter a 15 x 10 x 1-inch jelly roll pan. Cover the bottom of the pan with waxed paper. Butter and lightly flour the waxed paper. Spread egg mixture in the pan. Bake in

350°F oven 15 to 20 minutes, until puffy and lightly browned. Carefully turn out on a clean kitchen towel. Remove waxed paper. Gently roll up the omelet with the towel, rolling from the long side. Place towel covered omelet roll on a rack and cool a few minutes. Gently unroll and spread with hot filling, reserving a little of the filling for garnish. Reroll and cut into serving slices. Spoon some of reserved filling over each serving. Makes 4 servings.

Variation: Add one cup minced chicken or ham, or 1/2 cup grated cheese, or a cup of cooked, well drained, finely chopped spinach to the egg mixture before folding in the egg whites. Increase baking time about 5 minutes. Cold chicken or vegetable salad also makes a good filling.

PIZZA OMELET

Put your favorite pizza topping on an omelet.

1 tbs. olive oil
3 tbs. finely minced onion
1 can (8 ozs.) tomato sauce
1 tsp. oregano
salt and pepper
3 2-egg omelets
3 tbs. butter
sliced cheese
sliced salami or sausage
sliced black olives
sliced sauteed fresh mushrooms

Heat olive oil in small skillet. Saute onion 3 to 4 minutes. Add tomato sauce, oregano, salt and pepper. Simmer 5 minutes to blend flavors and thicken sauce slightly. Prepare eggs for three 2-egg omelets. Melt 1 tablespoon butter in

an 8-inch ovenproof omelet pan. When butter coats pan pour in one 2-egg omelet. Shake and stir until eggs are barely set. Spoon one-third of tomato sauce over eggs. Top with slices of cheese, salami, olives, and mushrooms. Put under broiler until cheese melts. Slide open-faced onto heated serving plate. Repeat for remaining two omelets. Makes three servings.

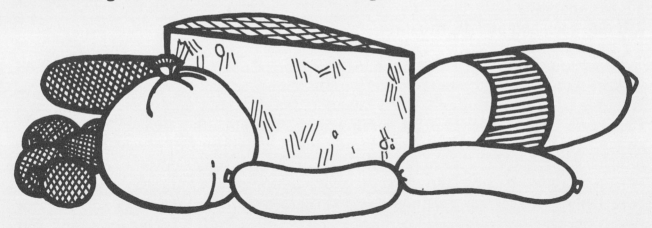

BACON AND TOMATO BREAKFAST SANDWICH

Strips of bacon and sliced tomatoes are layered between thin egg omelets and topped with avocado sauce.

2 tbs. butter
2 tbs. flour
1-1/4 cups milk
1/4 tsp. each salt and dry mustard

white pepper
1 ripe avocado, peeled and diced
6 slices cooked bacon
3 thin slices tomato

Melt butter in small saucepan. Stir in flour. Cook 2 minutes. Gradually add milk. Stir in salt, dry mustard and pepper. Cook, stirring until sauce thickens. Remove from heat and add diced avocado. Make 4 Thin Egg Omelets, page 59. Place one omelet on ovenproof serving plate. Spread with a little of the avocado sauce. Break 3 bacon slices into large pieces. Place on top of sauce. Top with another thin omelet. Spread with avocado sauce and top with tomato slices. Top with next omelet, spreading it with avocado sauce and remaining bacon. Top with last omelet. Pour rest of avocado sauce over. Place in 350°F oven for 10 minutes to heat through. Makes 2 servings.

BAKED ARTICHOKE OMELET

6 cooked artichoke hearts
2 tbs. olive oil
3 green onions, thinly sliced
4 eggs
2 tbs. pimiento, diced
1/4 tsp. salt
2 tbs. butter
1/3 cup grated Parmesan cheese

Cut artichoke hearts into small pieces. Heat olive oil in a 7- to 8-inch oven-proof skillet. Saute artichoke hearts and green onions 2 to 3 minutes. Remove from pan. Beat eggs, pimiento and salt together. Melt butter in same skillet and pour in eggs. Spread artichoke mixture over eggs. Cook until eggs have set slightly. Sprinkle with cheese and place in a 375°F oven 8 to 10 minutes until top of omelet has set and is lightly browned. Cut in wedges to serve. Makes 2 to 3 servings.

SECOND NATURE OMELET

For each 7-inch omelet:

3 ozs. Second Nature Egg Substitute
1/4 tsp. salt
1 tbs. vegetable oil
3 to 4 drops sesame seed oil

Combine Second Nature and salt. Beat lightly with a fork. Heat the vegetable oil and sesame seed oil in a 7-inch omelet pan. Pour in Second Nature mixture. Cook according to Basic Omelet recipe, page 8. Sprinkle with 2 tablespoons cheese or other desired filling before folding.

SECOND NATURE HERB OMELET: Combine 2 tablespoons chopped fresh parsley, 1/4 teaspoon sweet basil, 1/4 teaspoon chervil and 1/2 teaspoon chopped chives with Second Nature. Cook as directed.

Note: For fluffier omelets use 2 ounces Second Nature and 1 egg white.

PROVENCALE OMELET SANDWICH

This omelet filling also can be made into a frittata with the addition of 4 eggs; or use it in individual omelets, or as a crepe filling.

2 tbs. olive oil
6 to 8 fresh mushrooms, sliced
1 large onion, chopped
1/2 green pepper, chopped
2 zucchini, thinly sliced
4 Japanese eggplants, or 1/2 regular sized eggplant, diced
3 tomatoes
1 clove garlic, minced
1/2 tsp. dried sweet basil
salt and pepper
3 tbs. Parmesan cheese
2 to 3 tbs. grated Swiss or Gruyere cheese
2 Puffy Omelets, page 58

Heat olive oil in large frypan. Saute sliced mushrooms over high heat 2 to 3 minutes. Remove from pan and set aside. Add onion to skillet and saute 5 minutes until almost soft. Add green pepper, zucchini and eggplant. Cook 5 minutes. Peel, seed, and chop tomatoes. Add tomatoes and seasonings to vegetables. Cover and cook over low heat 10 to 15 minutes. Add mushrooms and cook uncovered another 10 minutes or until mixture is fairly dry. Stir in Parmesan cheese. Cook 2 Puffy Omelets in a 10-inch omelet pan according to instructions on page 58. Place one on warm serving platter. Spread with Provencale filling. Top with second omelet. Sprinkle with grated cheese. Place in 375° oven until cheese melts. Cut into wedges to serve. Yields approximately 2-1/2 cups filling. Makes 3 to 4 servings.

COUNTRY STYLE OMELET

A hearty omelet made with potatoes and served flat.

6 slices bacon
1 large baking potato
5 to 6 green onions, thinly sliced
2 tomatoes
1 tbs. butter
2 tbs. chopped parsley
6 eggs
2 tsp. water
4 drops Tabasco
salt and pepper

Cut bacon into small pieces. Fry until crisp in a 9-inch ovenproof skillet. Remove bacon and set aside. Peel and cut potato into 1/4-inch dice. Saute slowly in bacon fat. When almost done add green onions and cook until potatoes are lightly browned and onion is wilted. Drain excess fat from skillet. Peel, seed and

chop tomatoes. Melt butter in a small saucepan. Cook tomatoes over fairly high heat for 3 to 4 minutes until most of juice has evaporated. Spread potatoes and onion evenly around skillet. Sprinkle with bacon. Add cooked tomatoes and chopped parsley. Beat 6 eggs with water, Tabasco, salt and pepper. Pour eggs over potato mixture. Cook over low heat until eggs start to set. Lift around sides of the pan so the uncooked portion flows under the cooked part. Place under broiler as far away from heat as possible for 5 to 10 minutes until top is set and lightly browned. Slide out of pan onto serving plate. Cut in wedges to serve. Makes 4 servings.

Variations: Omit bacon. Fry potatoes in vegetable oil and use sliced salami, diced ham, thinly sliced Italian sausage, smoked salmon, or sardines.

Omit tomato and use 3/4 cup grated Swiss cheese, or Parmesan cheese.

In addition to onion, add green pepper, green chiles, pimiento and fresh sweet basil or coriander.

EGGS FOO YUNG

This is a Chinese-style omelet served with a brown sauce.

6 eggs
1-1/2 cups fresh bean sprouts, broken into 1-inch pieces
1/3 to 1/2 cup diced ham, small shrimp, or other cooked meat
1 cup thinly sliced fresh mushrooms
4 to 5 green onions, thinly sliced
1 tbs. dry sherry
white pepper
salt to taste

Combine all ingredients in large mixing bowl. Stir just until eggs are barely mixed. Preheat a 5- to 6-inch omelet or crepe pan with 1/4-inch of vegetable oil. Add one quarter of egg mixture. Cook until set. Turn to cook the other side. Drain on paper toweling. Hold in warm oven until other three omelets have been cooked. Serve with Chinese Sauce, page 75. Makes 4 large omelets.

CHINESE SAUCE FOR EGGS FOO YUNG

2 cups chicken or beef broth
1 tbs. soy sauce
4 tsp. cornstarch
2 tbs. sherry

Bring broth and soy sauce to boil in a small saucepan. Dissolve cornstarch in sherry. Stir cornstarch mixture into boiling broth. Cook until thickened. Makes 2 cups sauce.

DESSERT OMELETS

If an easy, light dessert is what you want, omelets are the answer. Omelets can be simple or elaborate, but never heavy. Especially pretty are flaming omelets. Lower the lights, pour warmed rum over prepared omelets and ignite. Your guests will love the effect.

Dessert omelets have sugar, cream and flavorings added to the eggs before cooking. The custard-like mixture is cooked in butter until the bottom sets slightly, then it is finished under a hot broiler. The filling can be as simple as jam or a fruit sauce spooned on the omelet before it is folded. Sifted powdered sugar dusted over the top adds a pretty finishing touch.

Fluffy, souffle-like dessert omelets make a glamorous appearance too. They can be filled and folded, or topped with a delicious sauce, garnished with nuts and cut into wedges. Serve on your prettiest dessert plate.

BASIC DESSERT OMELET

For each omelet:

2 eggs
2 tsp. sugar
1 tbs. heavy cream
dash salt
pinch of white pepper
1 or 2 drops (less than 1/8 tsp.) almond or lemon extract
1 tbs. butter
powdered sugar

Combine all ingredients except butter and powdered sugar in a small mixing bowl. Beat well with a fork. Heat butter in a 7- to 8-inch ovenproof omelet pan. When foaming add omelet mixture. Allow bottom to set slightly. Finish under a hot broiler until top is set and lightly browned. Fill with jam or other dessert filling. Fold and dust with powdered sugar.

VIENNESE DESSERT OMELET

Serve plain or fill with fresh fruit and cream, or top with a dessert sauce.

3 egg yolks
1 tbs. flour
1/2 tsp. vanilla
1/8 tsp. lemon extract

3 egg whites
1/3 cup sugar
2 tbs. butter
powdered sugar

Beat egg yolks with flour, vanilla, and lemon extract. Beat egg whites until foamy. Gradually beat in sugar. Beat until stiff peaks form. Gently fold egg whites into egg yolks. Melt butter in a 7- to 8-inch ovenproof omelet pan or skillet over very low heat. Pour in egg mixture. Cook until barely browned on the bottom. Place in a 350°F oven 10 to 15 minutes until top is puffed and golden brown. Slide onto serving plate. Fold over and sprinkle with powdered sugar. Makes 2 servings.

SECOND NATURE DESSERT OMELET

For each 7-inch omelet:

3 ozs. Second Nature Egg Substitute
1 tsp. sugar
dash white pepper
1 tbs. butter or vegetable oil
2 tbs. jam or jelly, or other dessert filling
powdered sugar

Combine Second Nature, sugar and pepper. Heat butter or oil in a 7-inch skillet. Pour in egg mixture. Cook according to directions for Basic Omelet recipe, page 8. Fill with jam or jelly and sprinkle with powdered sugar before serving.

Note: For a fluffier omelet, use 2 ounces Second Nature and 1 egg white.

BANANA RUM OMELETS

Here is a flaming dessert recipe.

2 large bananas
3 tbs. butter
4 tbs. brown sugar
3 tbs. dark rum
2 Viennese Dessert Omelets, page 79

Peel bananas. Slice in half lengthwise. Cut in half crosswise and then into quarters. Melt butter and sugar in skillet. Add banana quarters and saute until well coated with butter and sugar, approximately 1 to 2 minutes. Do not overcook.

Prepare omelets as directed. Divide banana filling and use one-half in each omelet before folding. Pour rum over omelets, flame, and serve. Makes 2 omelets.

APRICOT SOUFFLE OMELET

A puffy oven omelet topped with an apricot sour cream sauce and nuts.

Topping

1 can (16 ozs.) apricot halves
2 tbs. sweet sherry
2 tbs. brown sugar
1/2 tsp. grated lemon rind
1 tsp. lemon juice
1/2 cup sour cream
1/2 cup chopped nuts

Drain apricots. Reserve four apricot halves for garnish. Place remaining apricots in blender container with sherry, brown sugar, lemon rind and lemon juice. Cover and puree. Stir in sour cream and set aside. Prepare omelet as directed.

Omelet

6 egg yolks
2 tbs. flour
3 tbs. heavy cream
6 egg whites
2 tbs. sugar
2 tbs. butter

Heat oven to 400°F. Beat egg yolks with flour and cream. Beat egg whites until foamy and gradually beat in sugar until stiff peaks form. Fold egg yolks into egg whites. Melt butter in a 10- to 12-inch ovenproof omelet pan or skillet. over low heat. When foaming pour in egg mixture. Cook just a minute or two until bottom is slightly set. Place in oven 8 to 10 minutes until omelet puffs and browns lightly. Spread with apricot sour cream filling. Sprinkle with nuts and garnish with apricot halves. Divide into four portions and serve immediately.

MANDARIN ORANGE FILLING

1 can (11 ozs.) mandarin orange segments
1-1/2 tsp. cornstarch
2 tbs. sugar
2 tbs. Triple Sec
1/2 cup sour cream

    Drain orange segments, reserving juice. Place juice in small saucepan. Use 2 tablespoons of the juice to dissolve cornstarch. Add dissolved cornstarch and sugar to pan. Bring to a boil. Simmer, stirring constantly, until sauce thickens. Add orange segments and heat through. Remove pan from heat and stir in Triple Sec. Prepare dessert omelets and cook according to directions for Basic Dessert Omelet recipe, page 78. Stir sour cream into orange filling. Fill omelets with orange mixture before folding. Makes approximately 1-3/4 cups filling, enough for three omelets.

PINEAPPLE FILLING

1 can (8 ozs.) sliced unsweetened pineapple
1/4 cup brown sugar
1 tsp. cornstarch
2 tbs. dark rum
1 tbs. butter

Drain pineapple juice into small saucepan. Cut pineapple slices in half and set aside. Add brown sugar to pineapple juice. Dissolve cornstarch in dark rum. Bring juice to boil. Stir in cornstarch mixture and butter. Cook, stirring, until sauce thickens. Remove from heat. Add pineapple slices. Prepare and cook Basic Dessert Omelets as directed on page 78. Before folding fill with pineapple slices and a little of the sauce. Use remaining sauce for topping. Makes filling for 4 dessert omelets.

CHERRY BRANDY SAUCE

A good filling or sauce for dessert omelets. Try it with the Basic Dessert Omelet, page 78.

1 can (16 ozs.) tart red pitted cherries
1/2 cup sugar
1/8 tsp. cinnamon
1 tsp. lemon juice
1/8 tsp. almond extract
2 tbs. brandy
2 tsp. cornstarch

Drain juice from cherries into a small saucepan. Add sugar, cinnamon, lemon juice, almond extract and brandy. Bring to a boil and cook until sugar dissolves. Dissolve cornstarch in 2 tablespoons water and add to cherry juice. Cook, stirring, until sauce thickens. Stir in cherries. Use for a dessert omelet filling and topping. Makes filling for 2 to 3 omelets.

INDEX

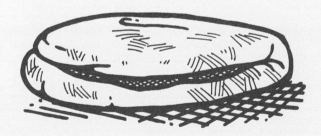